ALL BOOKS
Liam Gillick

Book Works
London

McNamara

Erasmus is Late

Ibuka!

The Winter School

Discussion Island/
Big Conference Centre

Literally No Place

McNAMARA
A script for a film produced from the notes made by a
reviewer staying in London in the early 1990s in the margins
of copies of various books. The final version of the script
was produced in four versions to accompany an exhibition
at Schipper & Krome gallery in Cologne in 1994. This was
the 'master'copy. A new script was written to accompany an
edition of three cartoon films produced for the exhibition and
originally shown on a Brionvega, Algol television. The main
characters are Robert McNamara and Herman Kahn of the
RAND CORPORATION. The focus on McNamara as a guilty
and complex figure predates the confessional tone of his
autobiography IN RETROSPECT (Knopf, New York, 1996).

McNAMARA A film

SCENE 1
TUNNEL
(McNamara/Kahn) *Torch/Music*

*It is day one of our story. We are in a complex tunnel system
under the White House in Washington DC during the early
1960s. It is dark and cold. Echoing footsteps are heard
followed by a torch beam. The emergent voices are those of
Robert McNamara, Secretary of State for Defense under JF
Kennedy and Herman Kahn of the* RAND INSTITUTE.
They are deep in conversation.

McNamara:
You know, there's a gap between his image and the
historical reality. Despite everything it's possible to re-work
a situation. That's why his popularity at home and abroad
reached super-high levels, even though we're talking about
a really short period of time.

Kahn:
Uh? (*Pause*) There's a contradiction here.

McNamara:
Concentrate Herman, we're right underneath this time.
The question of how to re-position is central to all this.

Kahn:
But the figures make everything seem so clear.

McNamara:
He reached a high of 83 per cent approval in the Gallup
Polls after that disaster and stayed within the sixtieth and
seventieth percentiles right through this year.

Kahn:
But nobody says percentiles Bob, nobody, not yet.

SCENE 2
MOTEL / INTERIOR
(Fiddle/Faddle) *Occasional traffic noise*

*Motel suite just outside Washington DC. Present are Fiddle
and Faddle, two young women who are clearly close friends.
The room looks slept in and the women are not quite fully
dressed. They move around. Restless but dreamy. The camera
pans around. Nothing is said for a while.
A peculiar tension builds up.*

Faddle:
What are you talking about?

Fiddle:
I didn't say it, he said it.

Faddle:
And I suppose that it all came from a book?

Fiddle:
Look, all he said was that Americans tend to equate good
looks with intelligence, sensitivity, sincerity.

Faddle: (*slightly sarcastically*)
Uh, huh—and self-confidence, independence, poise,
competence. (*Pause*) Hey! What about a dose of
inexplicable charm for good measure?

SCENE 3
TUNNEL
(McNamara/Kahn) *Music*

Cut back to the tunnel.

Kahn:
And what about good character Bob?

SCENE 4
MOTEL / INTERIOR
(Fiddle/Faddle) *Occasional traffic noise*

Cut back to the motel room. Close-ups this time. No music,
traffic speeding by outside.

Fiddle:
Did you ever meet that guy with the hair piece?

Faddle:
Oh God.

Fiddle:
Look, he talked to me about the way everything was
being treated. We're talking about full-scale persecution
by attorneys and private detectives. Let's face it, there are
cracks everywhere.

Cut to exterior shot of the motel.
Cut back to close-up.

Faddle:
So? Are you telling me something here?

Fiddle:
What language would you prefer? I can set you up with
a foreign-service officer who can tell you the difference
between a Donut and a city without moving his lips.

They both laugh but without malice.
Faddle mimes being a dog licking its lips. Up on the bed,
down on all fours.

SCENE 5
MOTEL / INTERIOR
(Fiddle/Faddle) *Occasional traffic noise*

We see the motel from the air and other motels like it. After some time we can still hear Fiddle and Faddle talking.

Fiddle:
Look, at least he experiments.

Faddle:
Yeah, with Mary-Jane, tea, pharmaceuticals and you.

SCENE 6
MOTEL / EXTERIOR
(Fiddle/Faddle) *Occasional traffic noise*

Camera re-approaches the original motel suite and comes through the door.

SCENE 7
MOTEL / INTERIOR
(Fiddle/Faddle) *Occasional traffic noise*

The two of them look calmer and are sitting side by side on the bed.

Faddle:
OK, OK... all the other things. all the other things. So... he hangs on to his mother.

Fiddle:
Keep it.

SCENE 8
TUNNEL
(McNamara/Kahn) *Music*

Camera to black, then we see a flashlight emerging through the gloom. We hear McNamara talking in a monotone drawl. Talking to himself although he is not alone. We are back in the tunnel.

McNamara:
One: Theo's dominant role in the creation of the book. Two: his Pulitzer Prize. Three: his Addison's disease and severe back problems. Four: the serious consideration of a first strike over Berlin. Five: total recklessness. Six: the cancellation of a television programme. An important broadcast. More important than any of us realised.

Fading now into the distance.

Seven: the relationship between the two of them and her. Eight: Camelot school behaviour. Nine: the claim to be a moral leader. Ten: the philosophy of natural law, which contended that there is a fundamental moral order of the cosmos and knowable by reason.

Music, getting louder, fading image to black. You can just make out Kahn mumbling.

Kahn:
Eleven: broken ambitions. A tightening of the throat. It's not going to work Bob. Sick to the stomach. (*Pause*) Bob? (*pause*) (*louder*) Bob?—Bob?

More music and flashes of light, footsteps in the distance.

SCENE 9
INDIA / INTERIOR
(Galbraith)

We hear a ventilation unit. The buzz of intense heat and the constant rumble, clatter and movement of a massive city. We are in a small room with a desk, a chair and a daybed. A man sits at the desk composing a letter. He is surrounded by papers and has three telephones. It is JK Galbraith and he is in India.

We take in all the details of a private study. Occasionally the camera lingers on a window revealing a sprawling city at dusk. The tall elegant figure of Galbraith sits at his desk, working hard. We hear his thoughts while he writes. Clarity at last, after the fragmented confusion of the earlier scenes.

Galbraith:
A few thoughts that I felt might interest you. Just remember all these things. The issue of character for one. Those 64,000 Irish who came over and all those Boston saloons, especially a particular east Boston bar. Remember PJ? You probably don't. In 1886 he was only 28. But within a few years he was moving along. Five consecutive terms in the Massachusetts House of Representatives, the State Senate in 1892 and 1893. What I'm trying to say is that much of his zealous pursuit of wealth resulted from a desire to show the proper Bostonians that he could do as much as them. Now, don't get me wrong, Rose echoed the resentment of her parent too. But they weren't alone. Many other lace-curtain Irish felt there was a large gulf between them and the back-bay Brahmins. I'm rambling, I know, but this important and I must get it down tonight. Anyway, the stock market in the 1920s was, as one historian put it, the close preserve of tipsters, insiders and manipulators.

SCENE 10
INDIA / INTERIOR / EXTERIOR
(Galbraith)

Galbraith breaks off from his work. Looks at his watch and gets up. We follow him as he prepares to leave the room. Then as he goes down the street we follow him across the city.

SCENE 11
MOTEL / INTERIOR
(Fiddle/Faddle)

Cut back to the motel room. Fiddle and Faddle are on the bed together. Top and tail. Each speaking to each other's feet. The radio is playing popular music.

Fiddle:
You knew that by 1924 he was a millionaire several times over, didn't you?

Faddle:
No. Is it important?

Fiddle:
It's real important. Not only that but the stock market and real estate speculations sorted everything out. You would have loved him. They were really building something.

Faddle:
Easy money. People drink right? Everyone could make more if they had some to start with.

Fiddle:
Some of us have never gotten over it.

Faddle:
And what about 'Doc'?

Fiddle:
He's got nothing to do with all that. We just do social events,
you know, country clubs, that kind of thing. He made
millions short-selling stocks during the collapse.

Faddle:
A real man huh?

Pause. We see that the television is on. No sound but various
images. The two of them are distracted by this.

Faddle: (*languidly*)
You know he was disturbed about the way his mother kept
going off like that. Especially seeing as he wanted her so.
And the father didn't help. Those crazy summer days. You
know what he told me? Family training camps. But get this.
He had a sister, Rosemary. She had a pre-frontal lobotomy.
They put her away. She ceased to exist. She was a loser.
There are no losers in this story. Not yet.

SCENE 12
TUNNEL
(McNamara/Kahn)

Cut back to the tunnel. Kahn has found a telephone on the
wall. He dials a few times but fails to get through and so
he keeps trying. McNamara is visibly agitated and whistling
occasionally.

SCENE 13
LONG ISLAND / INTERIOR

A house on Long Island. Inside the house the decoration is
conservative but comfortable. A phone on the table rings.
No one answers but the camera pans around. Silence is
punctuated by drones and creaks. All sounds are heightened.

SCENE 14
TUNNEL
(McNamara/Kahn)

Back in the tunnel. McNamara is digging. Sweating and out of breath.

McNamara:
You know Herman, you should never underestimate the power of a magical smile or a steely glare. Pass the bucket for me will you.

Kahn:
What are you looking for?

McNamara:
There are notes and there are notes. Not all the good stuff goes down on paper you know. Some of it goes right down. It's under our feet Herman.

Kahn:
You know he was in London for a year. I'm not sure about spellbinding smiles but if you're right about this, Laski's at the centre of things.

McNamara:
London School of (*pause*) Economics... there.

Kahn:
Laski took him to the Soviet Union?

McNamara:
Shit.

Kahn:
The Soviet Union? Bob. He took him to the Soviet Union. Let me look at that... It's OK... only a scratch.

We see the two from a distance fussing over McNamara's cut hand.

McNamara: (*calmer now*) (*close-up*)
You know, he grew up mostly afraid and in awe of his brother. Have you ever been leant upon Herman? It can affect everything you know. But it doesn't explain what's happening now.

Kahn:
Oh, I don't know Bob.

SCENE 15
MOTEL / INTERIOR

Rapid cut back to the motel. We move through to the reception desk and watch people checking in. Then pan to the bar and watch people drinking and talking.

SCENE 16
TUNNEL
(McNamara/Kahn)

Cut back to the tunnel. McNamara is still digging. Smiling occasionaly.

McNamara:
Whatever you think Herman. Fakey but undeniable. He would always hide his glasses from photographers. What about it? Blind as a bat but who'd want to corrupt an image like that. Where's the power. Top, bottom or middle, that's what we're dealing with here. Where's that power coming from?

McNamara is now in a sizeable hole. Kahn lights a cigarette.

McNamara:
You have to take notice at some point. Everyone will. We're looking at the only youngster seriously interested in books. Not only that...

Pauses for a few seconds and examines a blister.

What about it Herman? Is reading a form of escape?
Where's that coming from? Are we talking about emotional
damage or layers of control.

Kahn:
All of them are blocked, Bob. Totally blocked emotionally.

*They both laugh, while McNamara resumes digging with
renewed vigour. They are standing illuminated by a single
torch left propped on a pipe. Kahn is pacing around, clearly
attempting to resolve a number of issues and clues. We watch
them work for some time.*

SCENE 17
INDIA / INTERIOR
(Galbraith)

*Cut to India. JK Galbraith is in the shower. Thinking. Voice-over
accompanied by Indian instrumental music. We see steam
and the shower curtain from the study but do not clearly see
Galbraith at this point.*

Galbraith:
They were all blocked, totally blocked emotionally. At the
root of it were months of loneliness and their parents' often
selfish, insensitive behaviour. He grew up with a hostile
attitude towards marriage and the family. Women were at
best sex objects. I remember him saying to Clare Booth-
Luce: "Dad told all the boys to get laid as often as possible.
He used to say that he couldn't get to sleep unless he'd had
a good lay."

*Now we close in. We watch Galbraith while water runs off his
face.*

... Muckers club... who's the ringleader? Taking trips to a
brothel in Harlem for a first sexual experience... can't have

been more than seventeen. The white prostitute charged three dollars, that's what Bob told me. But what about his father's personal influence? No doubt it proved decisive. It had done at Princeton. Six foot and only 149 pounds. Less than intimidating. Attractive, sure—witty at times, yet unpurposeful.

Galbraith gets out of the shower, gets dressed, checks the room, picks up some keys, money, cigarettes etc. and leaves. Camera pans around empty room again and settles on a large pile of notes and papers. The same ones that McNamara and Kahn are looking for. The name Laski is clearly written on the top sheet.

SCENE 18
LONG ISLAND / INTERIOR

We see an aerial view of the house on Long Island again.

SCENE 19
LONG ISLAND / SHOP / EXTERIOR & INTERIOR
(Stranger/Shopkeeper)

Cut to a small shop. A man unknown up to now enters the shop. He buys some matches. Says hello in a pleasant manner and leaves again. The shop owner goes straight to the telephone.

Shopkeeper:
Bob? Well, where is he? Get him to call Sidney on the creek as soon as you find him.

SCENE 20
TUNNEL
(McNamara/Kahn)

Back to the tunnel. Kahn is now digging. Almost entirely out of the frame in an ever-deepening hole. McNamara looks exhausted and dishevelled. He is in shirtsleeves smoking.

McNamara:
You know Herman, I've been thinking about the background to all this. Within a short while his father was drawing fire as an outspoken isolationist and anti-Semite. There was that book. What was it called again? Something about sleep. Something to back up a nation. You know what they did to make the book a bestseller? How would you do it Herman? Why not just go and buy thirty or forty thousand copies. You could store them in the attic.

SCENE 21
TUNNEL
(McNamara/Kahn)

We see the extent of the tunnel for the first time as the camera backs off into the gloom gaining speed. We come right round in an arc and back to the two of them now both resting.

Kahn:
I give up.

McNamara:
But that's not logical or rational.

Kahn:
Anyway we all know how to get by without any training. Grant someone a commission. What about the Navy? Quite something don't you think. I wonder how he got that organised.

SCENE 22
MOTEL/INTERIOR
(Fiddle/Faddle)

Back in the motel. The room at first appears empty, then we hear muffled voices from a built-in closet. The camera approaches and we can hear Fiddle and Faddle talking in forced whispers.

Fiddle:
One of his conquests was Inga Arvad. She was really something. Could have been Danish. I can't remember. You know she was suspected of being a German spy. That was when he was in the navy. Ivy Leaguers who had yachting and boating experience always went for those little patrol boats.

Faddle:
So what?

Fiddle emerges from the closet holding a dress. She is alone.

Fiddle:
Well his efforts were heroic, especially in light of his physical condition. With all that boat business. The shame of losing 109 helped unite the crewmen behind him. It sounds pretty heroic to me.

Faddle appears. Not from the closet but from under the bed, clutching a red shoe.

Faddle:
You know he once typed me a letter. Filled with grammatical and spelling errors. It was about his brother. 'Cause you know what happened to him? Killed in an explosion. They were working on an experimental bomber designed to knock out V-1 launching ramps in France.

Faddle:
That Christmas at Palm Beach he got his orders. With his brother dead it was time to enter politics.

SCENE 23
TUNNEL
(McNamara/Kahn)

Back in the tunnel Kahn and McNamara are walking at some speed. We follow them, occasionally cutting to close-ups. Kahn's demeanour has changed. He seems more confident now. McNamara looks tired.

Kahn:
Let's get a move on.

They break into a trot.

Kahn:
I'm just filling his old man's shoes.

McNamara:
Yeah, with the money he was spending he could elect his chauffeur to congress. Some wags wore a twenty-dollar bill in their lapel and called it a campaign.

SCENE 24
HOTEL/INTERIOR
(McNamara/Kahn)

Cut to a shot of a hotel lobby. McNamara and Kahn appear in the distance, inexplicably emerging from a door.

Kahn:
Where's the third floor? What floor are we on anyway?

They disappear through swing doors.

SCENE 25
MOTEL/EXTERIOR

Fiddle and Faddle are having breakfast on the veranda of the motel restaurant. It is morning. Day two of the story. Fiddle is deep in thought. Faddle is attentive. It's an important confession.

Fiddle:
Well, if you really want to know, he started an affair with Gene Tierney—she was married to Oleg Cassini—you remember him? The fashion guy. Well, at the time the GOP was scoring huge victories. He was not forced to work out a meaningful political agenda or develop anything much. And you were talking to me about the qualities that have always been associated with tough leadership.

Faddle:
Well, I was only passing on what I'd heard.

Fiddle:
There was even a maid in his Georgetown home who reported to the ambassador, even though he was a frail sick yellow guy when I saw him first in 1947. It's not his fault you know. He always hated the backslapping that went with politics.

Faddle:
But what about those other guys? What did you call them? Young veterans. Nixon and Joe McCarthy, both elected to congress for the first time around then. They got along well with the strangest people. They were always just turning up. You must have noticed something.

Fiddle:
All I heard him say was this, and this is it, word for word. "I guess Dad has decided that he's going to be the ventriloquist, so I guess that leaves me in the role of the dummy." It's not so complicated. Even though the layers keep piling up. Everyone was obsequious as shit. OK, he's not such a tyrant but in his own way he's a bully just like his father.

Faddle:
What shall we do today? You want to go for a ride?

SCENE 26
MOTEL / INTERIOR & EXTERIOR
(Fiddle/Faddle)

Fiddle and Faddle leave the table and go through the lobby and out across the car park. Faddle stops and greets someone. We pan around taking in the scene. Finally they go to their room. They both grab bags. They are in good spirits. We follow them outside.

Faddle:
Shall we take the car?

Fiddle:
I'll drive.

SCENE 27
MOTEL / EXTERIOR
(Fiddle/Faddle)

They climb into a car and drive away. The camera follows their progress until the car can no longer be seen.

SCENE 28
HOTEL / INTERIOR
(McNamara/Kahn)

Hotel corridor. Kahn and McNamara are in the middle of a heated exchange. Due to the semi-public place they talk in harsh whispers.

Kahn:
But don't you see? It was a sophomoric approach to political ideology. The ambassador in turn knew what his son had to give his constituents in order to have a political future. The congressman repeatedly favoured fiscal conservatism and often expressed wariness about big government. That's why we're in this situation now.

The camera moves in to extreme close-up on their faces.

McNamara:
He backed the Marshall Plan. Both men were and are ardent cold warriors. He blamed the reds in the State Department for the loss of China. And don't forget that he had personally delivered his father's campaign contribution to Nixon for the Californian Senate race.

Kahn:
I know, it totalled $150,000.

McNamara:
You're following details Herman. You're not listening to what I'm really saying. There's a big picture and a mess of systems. We're right in the middle layer and you're not really listening to what I'm saying.

Kahn:
Well, it's not clear.

McNamara:
Look, I've been talking with Peter Milton and Lord Fitzwilliam.

Kahn:
What about them?

McNamara:
They told me about the priest who came aboard ship and gave Jack extreme unction. We thought he was finished then. But he keeps pulling through. Remember as recently as 1949, he began taking oral doses of cortisone. It's a hormone.

Kahn:
And you're saying it could have been tampered with?

McNamara:
That's more like it. Maybe, maybe not. We're looking further afield now. What we need is a specialist, but we don't have the time. He expected to die, Herman. Don't you realise what that means? He did, does and will always think that he is about to die.

Kahn is shaking with anger and cannot look McNamara in the eye.

SCENE 29
HOTEL/INTERIOR
(McNamara/Kahn)

The camera takes off backwards along the corridor. Circles round the hotel floor and returns to close up on McNamara.

McNamara:
OK, OK. We have an extreme case of delusion Herman. There are different ways of looking at this. One is a layered mess of coinciding circumstances. Alternatively, something's going on that we all know will end badly. And there's the possibility that he just had a congenitally bad back.

SCENE 30
EXTERIOR/DAY
(Fiddle/Faddle)

Fiddle and Faddle are in the car. The radio is on loud. They are both singing along with a romantic ballad, but they have changed the words, which now go like this:

Fiddle and Faddle: (*together*)
A formal announcement of his candidacy

and one day for the Presidency.
He labelled Lodge a socialistic New Dealer.
Lodge pleaded with McCarthy to help him out.
He was told now you'd be better of dead
'cause you helped the reds.
(*Chorus*)
The ambassador scotched Lodge
Oh Oh Oh
Made a personal appeal to McCarthy
and was always prepared... (*pause*)
with a sizeable donation.

They repeat the words in time to the song three times then the car grinds to a halt.

Faddle:
Dammit all.

Fiddle:
What are we going to do?

Faddle:
What are we going to do? What are we going to do?
Doing is what nobody is. Face it.

Fiddle:
Problems are solvable. Maybe we're the only ones who know what's going on.

Faddle:
Maybe so, but we can't stay here. Then again maybe someone will come and help.

Fiddle:
We have obligations now.

Fiddle motions to leave.

Faddle:
Don't go. Please don't leave me. This is stupid. Someone will come along in a minute.

Fiddle is already out of the car and making off down the road, looking back occasionally while Faddle starts singing the song to herself again, but quietly.

Faddle:
A formal announcement of his candidacy
and one day for the Presidency.
He labelled Lodge a socialistic New Dealer.
Lodge pleaded with McCarthy to help him out.
He was told now you'd be better of dead
'cause you helped the reds.
(*Chorus*)
The ambassador scotched Lodge
Oh Oh Oh
Made a personal appeal to McCarthy
and was always prepared... (*pause*)
with a sizeable donation.

Faddle sits alone in the car, the camera pulls away slightly to see she is sitting at a roadside. Cars and trucks are going past in the other direction and there is a large poster advertising a new business machine.

SCENE 31
INDIA / DAY
(Galbraith)

Back to JK Galbraith in India. It is an extremely hot day and we follow Galbraith along many narrow streets and passages. He is looking for a particular place. He can't seem to find it. Finally after some searching he looks up, checks a piece of paper and enters a very ramshackle building. We follow him up some stairs and he enters a small office. He enters, sits in a chair and starts to speak. He is obviously talking to someone but we never see or hear the other person. The camera stays fixed on Galbraith.

Galbraith:
Bobby, he was also arrogant, straight ahead. But no one

worked harder than his brother. Despite sickness he was still tough. They closely resembled each other on the campaign trail. And there were virtually no issues raised during the campaign—well nothing of any substance. There was a promise of new leadership. Vigour, forwardness and a new way. He was firmly on the road to the White House. But in the end something was missing. He lacked the full measure of his father's ambition. He wasn't as cruel and not as dominant. Lacking in focus, but friendly.

Lengthy pause—panning around the room but coming back to settle on Galbraith.

Charles Bartlett first introduced him to his future wife. A certain toughness and ambition was there and she wanted something better. He turned thirty-six a year later. Although he was old enough, marriage was his father's idea—there's no doubt about that. She wasn't sexually attracted to men unless they were dangerous like old Black Jack. Her private secretary told me in the strictest confidence that she was completely organised, always planning her life, always looking ahead. She was never naïve. So it came as no surprise to find that she disliked Rose's selfishness. Even going as far as to say that she was scatterbrained. Remember all that stuff about the Senate's Gay Young Bachelor?

Pause for reflection. Panning around the room, but always avoiding the listener.

He was often stunned by the bills pouring in after her shopping sprees. It killed him. But then maybe Ted could sort everything. Ted Sorensen, employed as a legislative assistant. Within a year articles were published in AMERICAN MAGAZINE, THE NEW REPUBLIC, THE NEW YORK TIMES MAGAZINE and THE ATLANTIC MONTHLY, all penned by Ted, but without his name on them. The junior senator from Massachusetts got a national reputation. He was seen as an important intellectual and an expert on public affairs.

Camera fades to black and then fades up again and pans round.

SCENE 32
CAR PARK/INTERIOR
(McNamara/Stranger)

We are in an underground car park. McNamara appears and looks for his car. He finds it, we see him get inside and start it up. He drives off at great speed. We follow the car out of the car park and along a series of fairly seedy streets. He turns many corners and appears to be taking the side roads rather than the main freeway that is frequently signposted. Suddenly, as he emerges from a side-turning into a larger street, without warning or build up, his car is hit by another one. McNamara and the other driver get out of their cars and start a heated conversation.

SCENE 33
STREET/DAY
(McNamara/Stranger)

McNamara:
Hey, you look like a smart guy, get this. You know, Sorensen was largely responsible for the wit, sophistication and literary prowess linked in the public's mind with the president.

Stranger:
Who cares? What about my car?

McNamara:
Your car, my car. What about a song? He always wanted to sing his favourite. Bill Bailey's WON'T YOU PLEASE COME HOME. That's the kind of guy he was. Don't you understand?

The stranger looks perplexed but is prepared to listen to more.

McNamara:
He tried to avoid the raging controversy surrounding Senator Joe McCarthy. You know he had actually dated the two Kennedy girls. Do you know what that means? Connections, buddy. Connections.

Quite a crowd is developing and the camera pans round their faces as McNamara continues.

McNamara:
We're talking about a strategic nightmare, a hastily designed and poorly thought out response to the ultraconservatives. It leads to a clampdown every time. This whole thing virtually outlawed the Communist Party.

The crowd cheers and McNamara seems to notice them for the first time. He raises his voice.

McNamara:
It was a 'double-fusion' operation. He received the last rites. Details of the operation were covered up, of course, to conceal Addison's disease. The press attributed his back problems to wartime service, linking the surgery with military heroism. He was the only Senate Democrat who failed to vote or pair against McCarthy. Principles or a principle for survival?

The crowd boos and hisses, some of them are laughing now.

McNamara:
You know? You wanna know one thing about Jackie? She was part of a prank that hired actress Grace Kelly to pose as a night nurse. When Jack opened his eyes, he thought he was dreaming. He received last rites for the second time. Jack had a hole in his back big enough for me to put my fist in it up to the wrist. I thought that pain had a shaping effect on personality. But all through this he was the handsome young war hero overcoming his disability with courage and determination. Improvements by endocrinologists in cortisone and its 'relations' gave him much of the strength he needed to pursue higher office. You can't watch a process like that and not feel something. Where to position, that's the problem.

We move away from McNamara to find him left alone in the street with his damaged car. The people have all peeled away.

McNamara:
How to reposition. What do you say to that?

SCENE 34
INDIA/EXTERIOR
(Galbraith)

Cut back to India. Galbraith is leaving the building where he was talking earlier. We follow him back through the streets towards his apartment. He looks either extremely disturbed or drunk or both. He goes up to his room, sits at his desk and starts writing furiously. We hear him in voice-over.

Galbraith:
Dear Jack,
Keep taking the weekly Novocaine treatments for muscle spasms. I know that Arthur Schlesinger Jr, James MacGregor Burns and Allan Nevins, Sorensen and Davids did most of the research and drafting of chapters for what became known as PROFILES IN COURAGE. And that Sorensen was responsible for the book's lucid and compelling style. I know you paid tribute to Sorensen as "my research associate". And I know that you claimed it was a book about faith in democracy, undaunted courage and "unyielding devotion to absolute principle". How did you try and reduce controversy over Stevenson's divorce. And what about all that poor health, youth and inexperience. I remember people saying "But he's a kid." I know that people like John Fox felt they had little use for you, thinking you were aloof and unreliable. And I know, as it happens, that the competitive drive and endurance that you had perfected in touch football served you well in the political arena. Like hell it did. While you were sunbathing one afternoon, a friend asked me why you wanted to be President. Without opening my eyes I replied "I guess it's the only thing he can do."

SCENE 35
HOTEL/INTERIOR
(Kahn/Barman)

Hotel bar. The same hotel as the one Kahn and McNamara entered earlier. We see Kahn at the bar. He is ordering drinks at a disturbing rate and talking to the barman. It is a confused story but the barman listens fairly attentively, or at least politely. It is clearly afternoon as the bar is quite empty. The barman occasionally takes time out to restock the shelves, whenever he can get away from the determined Kahn.

Kahn:
Give me another drink. Adlai's basic problem was his distaste for politics and politicians. You know that on election day, Bobby quietly voted for Eisenhower?

Barman:
Of course Sir.

Kahn:
Jack was especially intent on winning support in the south, a region certain to object to his Catholicism. And what about that old 'moderate stand on civil rights'.

Barman:
But...

Kahn:
But what? At the same time Jack's senate votes increasingly appealed to eastern liberals. Kennedy backed the most controversial and liberal section of the civil rights bill of 1957. Give me another drink... He followed a left-of-centre direction. Old loyal, clean and reverent. The democratic wiz of 1957. Clearly Jack was becoming politically astute and totally engaged. His old man loved it. You know what he said? This will kill you. He said "We're going to sell Jack like soap flakes." Yeah, but all the time this was going on Jackie detested politics. She was increasingly unhappy. Well, wouldn't you be too? Yet, all along Jack was developing into an above-average public speaker, and his beautifully crafted

addresses were all written by Sorensen—they were funny too. I'd call it a certain glibness. I'd never met somebody so completely obsessed with himself. Give me another. You know former Secretary of State Dean Acheson reacted angrily when Kennedy gave a speech advocating Algerian independence from France? I bet you didn't know that. And what about this? No other Democrat was making half the effort to win the presidential nomination. Of course no other Democratic hopeful had Kennedy's money. Give me another one of those drinks. He tirelessly flattered FBI Director J Edgar Hoover, whose files contained the Inga Arvad story and no doubt much additional information potentially damaging to the candidate. Ted Sorensen was the author of most of what Jack had to say. Give me another one. Let's drink to Ted. But let's drink to Jack too. Does anyone care about this? They're smears for sure, but someday it'll come out. It's no more than what's necessary.

SCENE 36
EXTERIOR / DAY
(Fiddle/McNamara)

Fiddle is walking along a dusty road. Somehow she appears to be in the Midwest but she has not walked so far. A fact that is revealed by a helicopter shot that takes off away from her and up into the air, revealing that she has only walked about a quarter of a mile. She flags down a passing car and gets inside. Camera cuts to inside the car. We don't immediately see the driver but Fiddle starts talking.

Fiddle:
What's your name?
(*Pause*)
Nice car.
(*Pause*)
Don't say much do you?
(*Pause*)
You interested in power?
(*Pause*)

Control?
(*Pause*)

What do you think about him? Cause if you ask me no
national figure had ever so consistently and unashamedly
used others to construct a reputation. There was so much
energy, I can tell you, so much money. But you know at
times Jack and Jackie were genuinely shaken at the poverty
they had to see, they were human too. Jack portrayed
himself as an all-out New Deal Democrat—a fighting liberal.
Judith Campbell had begun her affair with him. Frank Sinatra
introduced them you know. You ever go to Las Vegas? In
mid-March Sinatra introduced Campbell to Sam Giancana.
You don't say much do you?

SCENE 37
EXTERIOR/DAY

*Cut to outside the car. Suddenly we see the driver from outside
the car. It is McNamara. He is smiling to himself. Looking
straight ahead.*

SCENE 38
EXTERIOR/DAY
(Faddle/Announcer/Galbraith)

*We are back with Faddle again. She is still in the car at the
side of the road where it broke down. She slides across the
seat and stretches out. Turns on the radio and listens to a
programme of political analysis.*

Announcer:
Tonight on POLITICS IN PROGRESS we have a special
edition of the programme presented by JK Galbraith, the
distinguished economist.

Galbraith:
Tonight I'd like to get a few things off my chest... Bobby, he is imperious, ruthless, and unpopular. No one works harder than Jack. Despite constant back problems and bouts with exhaustion and nausea he is Kennedy-tough. The candidates closely resemble each other and there are virtually no substantive issues worth talking about. There is a promise of vigorous new leadership. Jack is now firmly on the road to the White House. But he lacks the full measure of his father's ambition, cruelty, and will to dominate. He is a more amiable, less focused man. Beneath the vigour, the expensive signs, and the slick slogans is little more than the desire to wrest power. Charles Bartlett introduced him to Jacqueline in May 1952. She was always tough and ambitious. Jack turned thirty-six in 1953. Marriage was his father's idea. She wasn't sexually attracted to men unless they were dangerous like old Black Jack. Her private secretary will write, "She is completely organised, always planning her life, always looking ahead." She is never naïve. Jackie dislikes Rose's selfishness and says she is 'scatterbrained'. Remember all that stuff about the Senate's Gay Young Bachelor? Jack is often stunned by the bills pouring in after one of his wife's frequent shopping sprees. But things get sorted out. He employed Ted Sorensen as a legislative assistant. Within little more than a year of his employment, 'Kennedy' articles were published in AMERICAN MAGAZINE, THE NEW.

Fading away at this point.

REPUBLIC, THE NEW YORK TIMES MAGAZINE and THE ATLANTIC MONTHLY. The junior senator from Massachusetts began gaining a national reputation as an important intellectual and an expert on public affairs.

The camera pulls back and we reflect in silence for a while on Galbraith's words.

35. McNAMARA

SCENE 39
HOTEL / EXTERIOR / EVENING

A car pulls up at the Hotel. McNamara and Fiddle get out. The car is taken by a hotel driver to be parked and they go straight into the hotel, past the bar. (Where we see Kahn slumped in the background) They ignore him and go into the closet. They enter the tunnel system. They walk some distance and nothing is said. Suddenly McNamara turns on her with a gun in his hand he orders her to start digging.

McNamara:
Just dig.

Fiddle:
But what with?

McNamara:
Use you hands.

Fiddle hesitates, but then complies. She gets down on the floor and begins scraping away at the dirt.

SCENE 40
EXTERIOR / EVENING

We see Faddle still sitting in the car. She looks visibly shaken by what she has recently heard on the radio. We only hear the announcer say that the same time next week there will be another programme of political analysis. She doesn't know what to do. She gets out of the car, looks around. Gets back in. Gets out again. Gets back in. Hits the steering wheel. Then stops. She tries the ignition. To her evident joy the car starts. She turns the car around fast in the street and heads back towards Washington. We see a sign saying Dulles Airport 10 miles.

SCENE 41
LONG ISLAND/INTERIOR/EVENING

We're back at the same house on Long Island. The camera pans around. Some things have been moved, a fact that would only be noticed by careful observers. The phone rings. No one answers.

SCENE 42
TUNNEL
(Fiddle)

We track along the tunnel system until we come across Fiddle. Dead and alone. There is no hole but there is evidence of a struggle.

SCENE 43
LONG ISLAND/INTERIOR/EVENING

Back to the house in Long Island. We see a static shot of the inside of the front door. Very slowly and very quietly we see a telegram slip under the door. It is not in an envelope. It is very long for a telegram and we close up onto the pages. It is the text that Galbraith had been writing in India. It is censored and only a few of the lines remain. As the camera scans it however we hear Galbraith in voice-over, so the text suddenly makes sense.

Jack,
Keep taking the weekly Novocaine treatments for muscle spasms. I know that Arthur Schlesinger Jr, James MacGregor Burns and Allan Nevins, Sorensen and Davids did most of the research and drafting of chapters for what became known as PROFILES IN COURAGE. Sorensen was responsible for the book's lucid and compelling style. I know you paid tribute to Sorensen as "my research associate". And I know that you claimed it was a book about faith in

democracy, undaunted courage and "unyielding devotion to absolute principle". How did you try and reduce controversy over Stevenson's divorce? And what about all that poor health, youth and inexperience? I remember people saying "But he's a kid." I know that people like John Fox felt they had little use for the aloof and often unreliable Kennedy. And I know that the competitive drive and endurance that you had perfected in touch football served you well in the political arena. Like hell it did. While I was sunbathing one afternoon, a friend asked me why you wanted to be President. Without opening my eyes I replied "I guess it's the only thing he can do."

SCENE 44
HOTEL / INTERIOR
(Kahn/McNamara/Fiddle/Barman)

Kahn is still slumped at the bar. He rouses a little as the barman calls his name. He looks at his watch. Suddenly he appears more sober and rushes towards the closet door. He is frantic and runs through to the tunnel system. He finds Fiddle's body. Checks for pulse etc. Then, after mumbling, gets up and runs on. Turning a corner he bumps into to McNamara running the other way.

Kahn:
Did you see the girl? Who did it?

McNamara:
I don't know. She was going to help me. She knows more than we do Herman. How? How does she know what's going to happen.

Kahn:
Kennedy and Giancana met secretly on April 12.

McNamara:
But she told me she's heard some FBI wiretaps. There's an Italian connection. It could spoil everything.

Kahn:
It'll make someone's life cruder Bob. But some stories are easier.

Suddenly and without warning Kahn swings hard at McNamara with a piece of piping. McNamara is wounded but manages to blurt out...

McNamara:
Giancana's daughter reported that the ambassador had promised them assistance against Federal probes. FBI documents that will be secured under the Freedom of Information Act will prove it.

Kahn leaves McNamara slumped on the ground, breathing hard and groaning.

SCENE 45
INDIA/INTERIOR
(Galbraith)

Back in Galbraith's room. We see him tidying papers and going through his desk. He is looking for something. He finds what he was looking for. It is a revolver. He loads it and takes aim at a photograph of the grassy knoll in Dallas. Shaking, he slowly turns the gun on himself as if driven by some overpowering force. He sticks the gun in his mouth and blows his head off (in slow motion). The camera pans away to blood-splattered notes. We hear Galbraith's voice (with echo) as we scan some of the papers.

Galbraith:
Both Jack and Bobby saw the tall Texan as their most formidable opponent. Plugging youth for youth's sake. Bobby was quietly wooing southern delegates by telling them that his brother approved of sit-in demonstrations only when they were 'peaceful and legal'. Since the sit-ins were already illegal, for the most part, southerners got the message and were pleased. He loved threesomes—himself

and two girls. He was also a voyeur. Bobby could usually be found directing strategy from the nerve centre. Precise, taut and disciplined. Bobby always spoke in commands. The contrast between the candidate's public persona of warmth, sincerity and ideals and the ruthless, heavily financed campaign that secured his victory could not have been greater.

SCENE 46
TUNNEL
(Kahn)

Kahn is alone now in the tunnel, but this time he is bruised and has blood on his hands. He is carrying a long piece of piping. He hears voices in the distance and we can see flashlights far away. He starts frantically bashing away at the roof. The flashlights are approaching. We can also hear dogs barking. Just before we can really see any of the people or hear what they are shouting, Kahn's work has the desired effect. The roof caves in on him. The camera frame is filled by ever-darkening soil and rock.

SCENE 47
TUNNEL / EXTERIOR / DAY
(McNamara/Cab driver)

McNamara, surprisingly clean and undamaged emerges triumphant from the tunnel into a park. It is bright daylight and the park is full of loving couples and people strolling around. He leaves the park, crosses a busy street and enters a bar. He orders a drink. He leaves the bar, hails a cab and asks to be taken to Dulles Airport.

He talks to the cab driver.

McNamara:
Take me to the airport.

Cab driver:
I've been thinking about this Kennedy guy.

McNamara:
I know him.

Cab driver:
You do? That's great. Shake him by the hand when you see him. Tell him it's from Giorgio.

McNamara:
I'll do that, I promise. But there are a few things you should know about the man inside.

Cab driver:
I know all that stuff.

McNamara: (*surprised*)
What stuff?

Cab driver:
Oh, you know. It was as though he is a new prince of peace and freedom. All that baloney. We all know that Krushchev's reply will be quick and friendly. The first time that red telephone rings, I bet Jack refuses to answer it.

McNamara:
If it rings at all, it will be a technical fluke.

Cab driver:
See? What did I tell you?

McNamara looks confused.

McNamara: (*unconvincingly and quietly*)
Don't worry, he'll give the conspiring Generals a green light.

Cab driver:
What did you say?

McNamara:
Oh nothing, just that I happen to know that Jack's final speech is packed with military data, anti-communism and appeals for courage to maintain freedom throughout the world.

Cab driver:
How could you know that?

McNamara:
Sometimes you're in the centre of things, even when you only wanted to watch.

SCENE 48
EXTERIOR / EVENING

The cab speeds off into the distance racing towards the airport. We follow its progress.

SCENE 49
AIRPORT / INTERIOR / EVENING
(Faddle)

A shot of the VIP lounge at Dulles Airport. We see Faddle enter the lounge dressed for travel. Her flight is called and we follow her as she moves onto the plane.

SCENE 50
LONG ISLAND / EXTERIOR
(Faddle/McNamara)

House on Long Island. Faddle and McNamara arrive together in a car. They sit together for a moment then proceed towards the door. We cannot hear what they are saying.

SCENE 51
LONG ISLAND / INTERIOR
(Faddle/McNamara)

We follow the two of them into the house. Faddle suddenly notices the telegram.

McNamara:
Give it here honey. Let me look at that.

McNamara stands in the porch reading the telegram while Faddle snuggles up to his shoulder trying to see what's written there. He holds it away from her in order to stop her reading.

Faddle:
What does it say honey?

McNamara:
Um? Oh, er nothing.

He crumples it up and puts the telegram in his pocket. They go through to the main room and sit in front of a large TV. McNamara sits in an armchair and Faddle sits on the floor at his feet. McNamara hits the remote control and we watch the familiar motorcade passing the book depository. Before we can see what is about to happen the camera pulls away from the set and turns on McNamara who is playing with Faddle's hair and looking contented.

McNamara:
When we look back on this in years to come I wonder what we'll make of it. Some people are inclined to dismiss warnings. No one entirely trusted McCone. They all thought he was self-serving. You know that he made repeated efforts early in the administration to convince businessmen of his support. The Kennedy administration's policies on taxes, trade and anti-trust were in harmony with corporate tastes. The president largely resisted the Keynesian appeals of Walter Heller and other liberal advisers. That's what I think's got to old Galbraith in the end. Honey? Honey?

The camera pulls away slightly to reveal that Faddle has fallen asleep. A half-smile on her face. McNamara sits back and is quiet. He is clearly exhausted.

Music/Credits

END

ERASMUS IS LATE
Set 'the day before the mob became the workers', this
book follows Charles Darwin's older brother Erasmus as
he walks around London in the 1990s looking for 'sites for
freethinking'. A Georgian opium eater displaced to the West
End. A group of people wait for him at a dinner in Great
Malborough Street, including Masaru Ibuka, co-founder of
Sony, Harriet Martineau, pamphleteer and friend of Malthus
and Elsie McLuhan, mother of Marshall McLuhan. The
book attempts to draw out the threads that lead towards
twentieth-century neo-Liberalism set at a notional point
where a form of eighteenth-century revolution in Britain
might still be possible. It is essential that Erasmus gets to
the dinner in time to engage with a pre-Marxist revolutionary
moment. Distracted and confused we instead follow him on
a meandering trail of half-thoughts and revelations.

ERASMUS IS LATE
INTRODUCTION

A dinner is about to take place. Tomorrow everything will be different. We are flashing between the early 1800s and 1997. For those stuck in the earlier period, the mob will become the workers. In 1997 the workers revert to their old identity. A group of people has been invited for something to eat. It is probably appropriate to explain a little bit about their activities. Robert McNamara was Secretary of Defense under Kennedy and later a World Bank representative. Masaru Ibuka co-founded Sony. Elsie McLuhan, mother of Marshall McLuhan, was a public speaker specialising in moral tales. Murry Wilson was the father of Brian Wilson. Like his son, he was a songwriter, but his ambitions were thwarted. Later he attempted to live out his desires through his son's band The Beach Boys. So it seems as if we are in the company of a specific collection of people. Maybe they would be seen as secondary characters by some people, but in this context their grouping at a dinner explains why there was no change at a specific period in British history. Not just any change, but a radical, revolutionary shift. There will also be a guide to London. A guide for freethinkers. An attempt to regain control over a set of ideas that have been appropriated by people with no interest in altering the way things are. All of this takes place within the framing device of a set of parallel histories.

So to the main subject of this book and the individual whose name forms part of the title. Erasmus is late, and he is the host. Charles Darwin's older brother enjoyed a life of literary leisure. A Georgian freethinking opium eater. We follow him as he wanders around central London. Despite the fact that he does not intend to let down his dinner guests, Erasmus gets distracted. For as he walks, he comes across different sites for the development of freethinking. At these moments he stops to contemplate the contradictions inherent in his desire for libertarian development. A set of problems that are amplified by the fact that the London he finds himself in is clearly a place familiar to us as the twentieth century draws to a close. It is no longer the London of opium eaters.

Although Erasmus has avoided his own dinner engagement, he maintains communication with his guests through this book. His new-found environment is too engaging to leave. This is not as much of a problem as it might at first appear. During bouts of opium-induced insomnia Erasmus finds that he can talk to the dinner guests and they answer him back. Yet if only he had arrived in time to meet them, everything could have been different. The London explored through this book might have remained the same, it is more likely that it would have been corrupted or even improved.

So on one level this is a guide to contemporary London through the eyes of a Georgian. Yet it is also an examination of pre-Marxist positions. An ill-researched investigation of a utopian optimism that is struggling to predict the future. An attempt to cut across the nostalgia for a period that cannot really provide a model for our own. The erosion of society as we never knew it, begins and ends here. Creating both the circumstances that lead to socialism and the roots of the present re-assessment of our sense of society.

Before we begin it is important to introduce Harriet Martineau. Older than Erasmus and not weighed down with the same sense of moral order. Her influence on his ideas should not be under-estimated.

CHAPTER ONE
A HOUSE IN GREAT MARLBOROUGH STREET

Erasmus is late. The table will have to wait. His insomniac wanderings have produced a guide to places that require further thought. A debate about the Other Man. A set of parallel histories. People coming together from a similar position but with separate starting points. Not so close in terms of what each person can achieve, but sharing an original connection that leads to debate. Skidding right through the centre rather than going around the outside.

There is a good story about China, but I cannot remember the precise details. The time of the 100 flowers. During the late 1950s Mao Tse-tung continued to develop his sense of revolution. At certain points he invited intellectuals, artists, writers and film-makers to contribute an ongoing critique of the state. At first people were reluctant to speak out, but once a few had begun to talk there was no way to hold back a complex web of proposals and suggestions. Through this process certain people revealed themselves. They were happy to come forward with ways to refine the revolution. In turn they too were refined. Destroyed or re-educated.

We are outside a house in London. Flashing between 1810 and 1997. Under consideration is a site for a meeting. Tonight in this tall, narrow home a group will come together and eat. Visit Great Marlborough Street and you will find the place. A basement may be reached directly from street level. The house is bounded by iron railings. One or two stone steps lead up to a shiny black panelled door. It is a place built from bricks. Bricks made from London clay. Mean, hidden window frames date it in the early 1800s. Some stone has been used. Not solid cut but a composite. This mix is patented and can be moulded for different applications. In this case the cast stuff tops the doorway and provides solid sills below each sash window. The roofline is hidden behind a low wall that extends up from the façade. Despite this the chimney stacks remain visible against the sky. Our house forms part of a terrace. Five storeys high. A light flickers in a second-floor window. This could be a comfortable place.

A space to occupy and enjoy a life of literary leisure. Erasmus is coming home. Tonight he will meet with parallel people, de-centred but necessary, even essential. And with his homecoming appears the possibility of refined debate. No permanent record will ever be left and no notes will be made. Erasmus is late.

Erasmus speaks to himself: "I am named after my grandfather and I have no archive. This is a story, not just a life but also a guide. You must be able to jump backwards and forwards across time in order to appreciate the information I will pass on to you. These time steps are not so hard to make and the process involved, while it causes problems for me, may not be so difficult for anyone else. In fact, some will find it the most straightforward form of engagement."

Harriet Martineau has been to the house many times in the past. Yet, now there is an element of disturbance in her usual pattern of settled dialogue. Apart from Erasmus, none of the other guests are known to her. And Erasmus has not even arrived. Harriet likes to be early and takes pleasure in the prospect of a new audience. But there has been a great deal of work recently and thoughts of moving to the Lake District. The dinner is not going to help. Tonight the guests appear to be uprooted. It is not the usual group. Maybe Harriet is just tired, but in mid-flow she can still talk and talk. For dialogue in this instance can be more accurately described as monologue. And Erasmus is late. He would always be here. It is his house. So Harriet picks up her ideas and starts to talk, regardless of such a central absence.

"If you want to understand the direction of this little gathering then you must accept that the desire to reject a form of total and continual change is hard to maintain within our desire for a particular form of libertarian dynamic."

The few guests who have already arrived look vacant. It is not important to try and read through in search of dialogue. For them it is a singular statement. Despite everything Harriet has begun to talk.

"It is quite possible that we are engaged in a search for multiple and shifting certainties in an effort to counter the heritage of our desire for stasis. Not only our desire for it, but its inevitability as a result of our former world view."

Harriet can speak as much as she likes. The other guests smile and acknowledge the one-sided conversation for what it is. They are more than prepared to enter into a debate but it will have to wait until later. Erasmus is walking along one of the busiest streets. A place for shopping. Somewhere to buy all the things he could want. Devices to help with communication. The shop has him mesmerised. The glow from the window lights his face. Erasmus continues along the road, deep in thought. Another shop window display catches his attention and leads to a reply. Harriet cannot hear but maybe the thoughts will not go unheeded.

"There is no reason to restrict this constructed vision to one particular period. An attitude that has become normalised but emptied of potential. A given web of overlapping set-ups. Something that you may have become used to. For me it is more difficult to conceive of such a rapid flickering without feeling its significance. I like to dwell upon future constructions but the context within which I work is weighted towards the acknowledgement of continuum. Therefore, what would be the point in trying to move through time? That would only expose a degree of progression that is predictable and true enough for my purposes while allowing justifications that result from the recognition of certain cycles of coincidence. I am caught and find it hard to deal with relativism, yet I am forced to begin attempts at positioning myself in your way. There is little point in thinking about the future when every day is the same. Spending long hours trying to prove daily similarities.

"But as we have discovered, days are not the same and if they are not even tied together by some thread of continuity, is nothing located? At least general trends might be predictable. That's the way it has been until now. Yet I fear that these undercurrents that permit a degree of rationalisation are merely coincidence. And on the trail of some opium I think even less in those fixed slightly progressive terms. I am permitted to time slip into your mode of multiple referencing. But it is not your theoretical freewheeling, my version of multi-vision merely apes a-historicism. No cultural kleptomania. My time slip is based on what could be and not on some existential set of total referencing that may lead to inactivity."

The traffic flows in one direction. There is no real break.
The vehicles are indistinct. Darkness on the road is peculiar
given the number of shops here. But for Erasmus there are
four more glowing retail sites to visit and the first lies across
the steady stream. Still caught in the reflections of the non-
debate with Harriet, there is no urgency in his movements.
The priority stands on the other side. It was the signage that
first attracted his attention. The vast number of logos in the
form of names. The choice of such names often came about
through the desire to create something understandable
across many borders. Ibuka knows all about that. But will
the availability of various components, all connected to
recording discussion provide any kind of answer for our
guests? The appeal of the stuff is clear enough but Erasmus
did not remember the places ever having been there. It is
clear that something is taking hold of him. There is a feeling
that the dinner tonight is taking place at a crucial moment.
It is a question of naming. And the signs are all part of that.
Erasmus is standing in front of a projection that
encompasses future profits and a desire for market share.

In the house. A dark, narrow hallway. A staircase leads
straight up from the front door. A passage twists around the
plain dominance of the sweeping stairs and takes you
through to the back of the building. Upstairs. The second
floor is faintly illuminated. Some activity is taking place with
sounds of conversation. The interior is too dark to allow full
view of the decor. But it's only early evening. A few people
have gathered but the central character is absent. They sit
around a heavy table. Its surface lightened by a clean white
cloth. Harriet has been speaking but now she is silent. A
mantelpiece carries photographs, drawings and a small pot.
None of the people pictured there are recognisable and the
ceramic is hard to date. Erasmus is coming.

"There are social constructions to think about and practical
developments to discuss. So we accept that much has been
made of my contemporaries' attempts to rationalise through

observation, travel and work. But I will lead you into territories too distinct to bear. All this without leaving the immediate vicinity of my Great Marlborough Street home. My friends are paving a way for your controlled markets and protecting their intellectual investments. I remain uninterested in a situation where man develops fitness. Fitness for a particular function is open to variance and chance as much as to self-determination. As developments take place they are constantly wrecked and corrupted. In light of all this it might be interesting for me to be your guide towards a world of unfitness and under-achievement. I need to revel in such a breakdown of progress. If this guide is to work, it is important to recognise the significance of non-structure. Replace it with a state of consistent re-consideration. Yet while I revel in the free-form, I too require some starting point from which to embark upon my mental excursions."

Caught within the window light, scanning the single-word company names: "So my text is neither strictly historical nor contemporary. Yet it is uninteresting to become involved in a fetishisation of indecision. That is not what this book is about. We are dealing with the absent presence of ideas. It is not a case of multiplicity and the potential of doubt. We are engaged in a faded analysis."

Still waiting to cross the road Erasmus interrupts his thoughts in order to snap the waiting guests from their comfort.

"One option here is for us to chase a consistent level of ongoing invention. This is supposed to occur anyway and, while change has been slow, it has not been imperceptible. Certainly when keeping in mind what goes on beyond the kind of discussion that tends to take place at a dinner like this. Maybe, concerning what was said earlier, we are in fact taking part in the construction of a whole new series of tiny moral frameworks that guide our actions instead of some grand, overwhelming and therefore rather clumsy idea. This proposal would seem reasonable, seeing as it is always being adapted by the most dynamic people, although to link ourselves with such groups may be dangerous at this stage."

In the middle of the road. A tall man with watery eyes. Hair swept back off a high, lined brow. Bushes of grey hair framing loose-lipped concentration. Erasmus remains caught within the attraction of the shop windows. Stuck, unable to complete his crossing. Standing on a traffic island. Thinking.

"I am in the middle and I function as a conduit for what has happened and what might be possible. I am the Other Man. There is no reason for me to travel and no reason for me to look too closely at the formulation of rational theories in relation to production. At this stage, getting anything produced at all could be enough. Not consumer items but a set of guiding principles that, once identified, could allow some form of revolution to take place. For tonight the mob become the workers and after this point all the procedures with which to abuse power structures will be irrevocably altered. For now, for just one night, everything remains. Laid out, layered and compressed. At this moment I have my theories and my sense of what could be. All I know is that it is necessary to create debate. Discussion has been closed for so long. I want to develop sites for freethinking and resurrect some from my youth. These locations surround me but they need to be connected. They are specific but also intangible.

"So instead of particular vagueness, what do I remember? That there is one brother and two sisters. But I have no parents and I have no children. Certain issues are denied so I look elsewhere for inspiration. From the earliest point I have been aware of the possibilities of free thought. And the additional thought that is barely memorable yet astonishingly clear when caused by the passage through a narcotic haze. For the last two weeks I have been dreaming of a drug-induced condition that would allow me to face the massive shift that I feel is about to take place. Looking for new ways of moving around. I remain trapped here but think of how to slip along closer to the ground. Snaking below the shop windows. That's a possibility. A new kind of sport that has never caught on. Wearing an adapted wetsuit, and slithering across all terrains. Swimming in the sea, crawling through the backstreets. Avoiding the clarity of attraction.

"In these brightly lit windows there are some objects to buy that appear to have electronic possibilities. The chance to record a book. And the first opportunity for me to possess debate. But I can hardly move and would certainly fail in any attempt to articulate my desires for these objects.

"I have a problem. It is too hard for me to work out what might happen tonight. I need a model to aid my analysis. Maybe it is a question of trying to examine the communicative abilities of captive animals in the same way that it might one day be possible to take apart human communication for the purpose of study. Perhaps that might help me to establish a model with which to negotiate this evening. The idea of zoo-semiotics passes through my mind as I stand considering five sites of electronic communication in Tottenham Court Road. It is possible that the application of such an overview to a situation that may not be predicted will not help me in the least. But in the first instance it may present a useful diversion. Yes, a trip to the Zoological Society can produce interesting results in the middle of a sleepless period."

In the house the other guests have arrived for dinner. A Canadian, two Americans and a Japanese sit with Harriet. The Canadian is a woman in her forties. Sharply dressed with a precise demeanour. Her contributions to the conversation are specific, carefully worded constructions. Metaphorical rationalisations of behavioural morality. She sits upright and concentrates on the potential pleasure of such a social gathering. To her left the Japanese gentleman appears to be somewhat disorientated. He is more used to spending time alone rather than devoting his attention to meetings. Regardless of the importance attached to coming together for pleasure or to define strategy and possibilities. They sit together, Elsie and Masaru side by side.

At one end of the table is a dark-haired man wearing glasses. Bob is clearly in need of a break. McNamara is with the others but stacking alternative possibilities and scenarios. Yet he always deals with the situation at hand. That's his strong point. By now we are all aware that certain time slips are taking place. There is no chance that Harriet could really sit with such a group but there she is. And Erasmus is coming. Only podgy Murry, propped up by the fire, seems truly delighted. Not sure of what is going on but certain that he has found his place. Humming a stupid tune but following the interchange as it begins to develop. Murry thinks of possibilities in a limited way.

Less than a mile away, Erasmus has escaped the lure of communication and is heading south.

"I am no more interested in your modern world and its ironised responses than I am in any period or any social set-up. There is no difference for me between the manifestations that dominate one particular time and the constructions that overwhelm the next. There is every difference for everyone else. I am viewed through a haze but I am not suffering from cloudy vision. I have created a precise way of reconsidering the notion of clarity. The places of discussion and the places of learning are heightened for me in a way that is hard to express. My memory is so long and my projection into the future has reached so far. For while the world has been taken apart, the analysis of what has been broken down is wrapped within a web of near truth. On top of this is the possibility that I had already reached a series of conclusions without the necessity to travel or even to leave my place of thought."

Murry picks up a small, decorated jar from the mantelpiece. He weighs the delicate pottery in his fat fingers. Looks inside. Sniffs, then carefully replaces it. Masaru is smiling at him.

"And Mr Wilson?"

Murry flushes and glances across at McNamara. Seated and expectant, the small group is not intimidating. On the contrary, it would give them great pleasure to open things up. Murry. Why is he even there? Not something to worry about. Think of an answer. Smiling back, this time directed at Elsie, Murry asks about the production process that led to the creation of the jar he was so recently examining. OK, so the faces fall every now and then, but it was a sincere question. His intentions are fine. But not abstract enough to pleasure this group. But there's a point to be made here about industrial process, benevolence, hope and projection. Murry can feel it but it is beyond his expression. Masaru believes it, but it is so central to his progression that an opening remains unexplorable for now. He cannot see the potential in Murry's simplicity. Elsie turns away, embarrassed by the exchange. She draws small circles on the table top with her middle finger. Hypnotic and revealing. She wants Bob to break everyone out of this temporary stasis. She is drawn to him but disturbed by the extent to which he seems to be in the middle of some moral, yet unspecified, personal crisis. De-centred association with and tolerance for a set of ethical positions that she cannot read. Bob looks up. He has been thinking.

"I know it seems difficult to accept, but it is important to consider the relation of the individual to a whole set of apparently imprecise constructions that, while difficult to identify, clearly have an overwhelming effect on the way we interpret behaviour. Make no mistake, it is possible to enter into such a quest for analysis. The results of any search quickly become fixed markers in any future course that attempts to chart its way through the various potentials that we are faced with. And some people have reached that stuck, locked, immovable, static ability to capture everything. But the whole course is fuelled by frustration. Frustration with a set of analytical tools that are bent and deformed. Because the people who use those devices appear content to merely reprocess an overload of cultural signifiers in a state of hypnotic reverie. The answer for a few people, those I would not call my friends but whom I am fascinated by, is to quit the role of spectator within the spectacle and start becoming part of the paradox and not just an observer of its effects. I have been trying to find a way to live, a way to contribute to the incorporation of government and how to affect the management of social programmes. Whatever way you look at things it has become almost impossible to escape the symbolic and metaphorical quality of the best analysis. I know, I've tried."

Masaru, staring intently at the floor.

"I have heard of a proposal, a set of proposals, predicated around the creation of a number of centres. Places where practical demonstrations can occur. Encouraging the exploration of ideas and proposals within a setting that acknowledges the dominance of spectacle, unprocessed and direct. Connected to your appreciation of Malthus. All of what you say is still based upon a combination of ideas derived from a peculiar moment in history. A legacy of non-conformism that has many connections to my way of thinking."

There are parallel activities. These varied engagements may be carried out by people capable of noticing temporary gaps in the construction of society. Entering those ill-defined spaces and mimicking the activity of close neighbours. At first such proximity may disallow the chance to read that parallel activity as separate from any other. Yet the necessary adoption of such positions is central to any true analysis of the state of affairs as they may be found at any one time. It sets up the beginning of parallel histories that permit the creation of a number of new possibilities. The trick is to know when to get in and when to get out.

Erasmus is a parallel historian. No longer involved in parallel activities, but capable of understanding what they can achieve. Gone further south, away from the shopping centre in search of a set of justifications for his earlier activities. An examination that crosses various periods and leads towards a corrupted sense of trajectory. Walking with a purpose now. Turning off the main north-south road. Maintaining the general direction but complicating it by swift strolls up and down back streets. There are reasons for this behaviour. Avoiding the crowds and creating more time to think.

"I have drunk not only opium but also become stuffed with other people's ideas. I need time to absorb them properly before re-engaging in a night of debate. Although in general it is better to avoid the use of the word 'idea'. Maybe I will convey my meaning with greater clarity if I refer to my thoughts as 'in-senses'. This renaming is due to the origin of such thoughts, but also refers to the basis of their analysis. All the ideas that I process are subjected to a combination of opiate reverie and a Georgian life of literary leisure. Each one framed by a love of suppers. For there are opportunities for travel now in our expanded empire. Given the abstractions that restrict clarity, an over-familiar notion may be as useful to me as it is useless and under-used by you. At every point, however, the question of an archival sensibility is brought into play. It deserves attention, because at the heart of any progress is a desire to create a certain degree of empirical reckoning. At least it may seem that way later on in my meeting with the others. This desire is purely in order to accommodate their thinking, and to allow me to truly engage with a number of secondary people across time. All these dinner guests rely upon a degree of deterministic thinking, it's not such a bad thing, but it denies a true recognition of the potential inherent in the gaps. Not so much "which side of the barricade?" as "which barricade?" I am fascinated by the increasing tendency to refer to every set-up in terms of the (apparently) scientific. Or the quasi-legal. Obviously, these are ways to approach things but what confuses me, and what I must be prepared for, is the possibility that the others will be acting in a manner that is overly conscious of the desire not to act in any way that reveals too much allegiance to such a lucid set-up.

"Multiple positions are difficult. Despite the fact that I appreciate their potential, I am not sure that I can quite find the energy to locate myself as a barricade seeker. And all of this is complicated by the fact that I have no archive. It is of little importance for me to chronicle the shifting frame of events. The problem with this is it also makes it very hard to keep a true record of what is going on. This ensures that I have no feeling for decision-making and the application of laws to various situations. It may be the starting point for my friends, and as such may help them to back up an argument. Remember their need to re-jig the rationalisation of constructions that will possibly devastate the closely held and cherished beliefs that permeate and support my situation in early Georgian London. But perversely it is not a route open to me if I am to maintain the true essence of freethinking. I cannot use the tools that are available to other people yet. Mainly because I am talking from a pre-Marxist position. Under attack for the moment, but hopefully avoiding the kind of action that will lead to the worst kind of short-term solutions. In my time the accepted model of a world in which everyone knows their place can still be undermined by freethinking. The barricade has not been erected yet. The battle lines have not been drawn. People are not quite sure which way things will go. What will be the effect of education on a large proportion of the population? Do people tend to pull themselves up by the bootstraps?

"This must go hand in hand with a careful gaze. Ensuring one does not look too closely at the changes going on that are the result of libertarianism. The utopianism that I am seeking out absorbs many possibilities. A more precise analytical position, rooted in science, is one that appeals to me, but is set up for others truly to take advantage of. I can formulate propositions and I can liberate the modes of discussion, but I am lost when it comes to cataloguing or accurate cross-referencing. No, that is not entirely true. A degree of comparison can be elevating, but in my case it has to be carried out in a way that encompasses a certain amount of freedom combined with a lack of precision. For in this case, it takes place with no notes or archives. Yet my non-existent archives also deserve attention. While they are absent, something parallel has replaced them. Maybe the substitute is a series of synaptic connections that, by their very nature, can endure no consistent labelling. A frequent dousing in chemical compounds waters them and leads me to all conclusions and endless propositions. As such it could be said that I have entered into a spirit of consultation with my non-archives that has allowed my in-senses to predict certain developments and discuss various possibilities. All these things allow me to read different time frames with equal clarity. I can consider the past, the present and the future with ease. In fact, at times, it is true that none of these terms hold any meaning for me any longer."

Erasmus is standing, still, caught within his thoughts. Buses and cars stream past but he remains oblivious to the incongruity of his presence among the commuters of the mid-1990s. He thinks on.

Masaru is standing now. Having taken Murry's place by the fire. Over and over in his head he keeps hearing the word "Angus". It repeats "Angus, Angus". Then music. Something must be said.

CHAPTER FOUR
A NIGHTCLUB IN CHARING CROSS ROAD

Erasmus is still thinking. But is he getting anywhere?

"There is a need to respond effectively to your desired control of communication. I acknowledge your recognition of the apparent transparency of the sites for debate. And when I talk of you, I don't just mean the people waiting for me, I am referring to all the others who will have to come to terms with the legacy of libertarian development. And all the time I am aware of the fact that even the most radical re-definitions of how we begin talking about things tend to be caught within the truth that the potential of a group of people coming together across time is high, but what they might actually provide is something else altogether.

"A later argument will be that the most interesting activity embodies a set of guidelines that are apparent within the physical quality of the result. To a certain extent this applies to both state control and apparently more transgressive groupings. Leading to an argument that justifies any behaviour as acceptable while debate functions as a separate commentary upon wider territories. Debate indicating a series of signposts and allusions to a chaotic situation. Yet a shift has taken place. A refinement of the familiar arguments. There will be a resurrection of talk about where you position yourself, going beyond or not recognising the traditional sites for discussion and trying to ape the complexities of the socio-political landscape."

Think of a nightclub, any nightclub, somewhere to go in the centre of London towards the end of the twentieth century. A place to watch and feel part of a continuing exchange of visual references. Harriet looks up:

"You said, 'Leading to an argument that justifies any behaviour as acceptable?' "

Erasmus can hear her, even though he is now standing outside a solid door. This entrance way is overlooked by a closed-circuit camera system. "I am a freethinker and I have eaten opium for ten years. Some say that this is etched on my face but the truth is that my face is etched over the city. For other people it is a new landscape. Barely recognisable. Yet there are behavioural patterns that remain clear. Compounded by theoretical constructions that I can appreciate. There are systems and modes of interaction that I am familiar with, but they evade critical focus. I spent many happy evenings in conference with my friends and I thought of many possible frameworks for this guide. All of them had their limitations. Yet they are sufficient. Don't forget the melancholia that comes from sleeplessness. Not at first, but on reflection. I know that my brother will travel and visit many different places. He is not yet sure of the route. I know what his travel will provoke. There is limited use in advance warning or speculation. It is not necessary to ask where I got this knowledge from, it is sufficient to trust me. Believe in what I am doing and follow me on my lengthy journey over the shortest of distances."

Joy Division, survival of the fittest. The simple version of what happens when you take that attempted rationalisation its full course. How do people develop? How could you control what they become in the future? If people change, adapting to their environment then why not help that process along. I'm sure he didn't mean it to be used that way.

Erasmus thinks on. "I have just eaten a large lump of the purest opium and am getting ready to depart. First consider eight places. They are all locations for thought. Ideas are linked to these sites. There are no specific addresses at this stage. Just vague indications that allow the reader a chance to travel guided by the book. Towards these locations are different routes. Some of these ways encompass other places where people and ideas may come together.

"I enjoy the idea of sitting with a number of people and talking about possibilities. Although it might be more accurate to say that I would prefer to be at home asking the questions rather than stuck out here on the streets. Maybe it's true that a discussion of this sort really leads towards a degree of disorganisation. We have entered a perfectly chaotic environment. And are ready to face the ultimate interaction. Debate that leads to no conclusions but merely offers signs pointing towards more debate. An allusion to what might be possible hidden within an enjoyment of talking. Yet there is fear mixed in with this pleasure. And it is possible that I have recently witnessed a profound alteration of intention.

"Certain repeated arguments have become somewhat purer in the hands of people who feel that they have some kind of rational structure with which to moderate their ideas. Their position may be supported by an emerging professional class. At this point we are in a Georgian environment, so all of this analysis is still hidden behind a cloak of amateurism. But do not let this deceive you, all the necessary elements exist to push forward with a total readjustment of relative social positions. At some point, however, after this has taken place, it will become clear that constant adjustment of status will be necessary. Discussion always centring on the subject of where you place yourself. The traditional sites for discussion will be even further clarified. The fetish will stretch to embrace every type of activity. No business will be possible, and no analysis will take place."

Murry is getting into the swing of things. But he is not quite sure what Erasmus is talking about. Something to do with the way in which potential may be discarded. A fear for the future but an acknowledgement of the fact that the ride has begun and there is no way to stop.

He's humming a stupid song.

CHAPTER FIVE
BACK IN TOTTENHAM COURT ROAD

Now in the sidestreets. Lingering to check a final window? Just on the point of moving into Charing Cross Road.

Erasmus is smitten with his multi-layered analysis. His avoidance of the dinner engagement causes him no guilt. On the contrary, avoidance of the issue at hand is crucial if what he really fears is to be avoided. That final shift into a totally manipulated revolutionary position could take place tonight, in the morning it will be too late. Harriet has already spoken about moving to the countryside, and once the workers have assumed a self-identity it won't be possible to play with them any more. So there are more and more geographical diversions. Ways of avoiding things but also permitting the creation of an elaborate metaphor.

"Although this is a guide to what already exists and what has existed in the past it must also look towards future possibilities. These are the most difficult concepts for me to resolve. Stresses across time are very hard to deal with. They are exhausting and using up my limited strength. Yet I am Erasmus and I am relaxed and it is important that I stay that way. It helps when considering what might be possible. For a while it seemed as if there were eight places within reach but now it appears that there are definitely twelve locations that require visiting. But there are also many ways to get there. The separate routes or directions are not clear at this moment. They might represent people, places or ideas. I will keep you informed of my progress and let you know where we are led. The structure is clumsy and it may spill over. I will attempt to retain a degree of guiding rigour but there is no guarantee that I will not reframe it later on."

Futurology. The key to everything is an understanding that a desire to predict the future is central to the development of a particular form of free-marketeering. A focus for progress. But a process that can happen in reverse, become mythologised or even forgotten.

Elsie speaks clearly with the trace of a Scottish 'r'. "What are we really looking for? I would suggest that there was more than just a little play and, dare I say, desire, under the surface. We remain stuck inside a set of contradictions that require some analysis. I have heard you say in the past that these contradictions always existed and were merely ignored. But does this not imply that we cannot know if they ever really existed in the first place? To have an extended discussion between people over time, something about the very nature of discussion itself will obviously begin to overwhelm the subject any of us might be attending to. So we disagree. And if we have any level of accord it might be because we recognise the power of paradox. Attention to detail is becoming the key mode of behaviour. And as this concentration on smaller and smaller elements increases so it will come under attack from a social system that uses the power of contradiction to keep shifting the goal. This will be of some use to Erasmus's free-market relatives."

So many concerns exist that you have to rely on fragmentation and layering as a central element when analysing the most interesting recent possibilities. This informs those who are interested in society and decoding its messages. A proliferation of multiple activities is revealed through the tension that arises when attempting to deal with some of the following aspects of the formation of society now. For example, the tension between intention and results, attempts to define a social role opposed to the powerful dynamic of free thought, issues of sexuality and gender in light of discrimination, issues of identity in the face of exclusion. Most notably there is the inevitable absorption of attempted radicality within an apparently insatiable world. On top of this apparent earnestness it is necessary to pile irony, self-knowledge and layers of complex referencing. How to reclaim the territory of dynamism without resorting to a competitive structure. Or, more accurately, how to create a competitive structure that allows for sympathy. Big stupid questions that Erasmus feels responsible for. Maybe it's the opium cutting in.

Sometimes no one speaks. Back in the house, time passes slowly. Maybe it is the best moment to begin our guided tour. Then again, we are nearly half-way through it. It might be more accurate to say that it is time to assess where on earth Erasmus thinks he is heading. Everyone is ready and the places are open and waiting for us to arrive. But he has no memory of how many sites there are and no desire to look them up. No desire to travel and to check if the numbers are correct or appropriate. It is sufficient for these purposes to establish the locations. They can act as symbolic conduits for an investigation of freethinking.

Consoles will be developed that allow interaction with machinery and markets. Consoles are the key. Not just in their late-twentieth-century form. A simple set of handles will suffice. As much as it is interesting to focus on the machine itself or on general principles of capitalism, I find it equally useful to look at the tools with which these things may be operated.

Rather than just thinking, Erasmus also talks to himself. "My best friend is Harriet Martineau. In many ways she is more precise and radical in her views. She is certainly the most profound influence on my thinking. I do not always agree but am continually affected by her position. Yet you must be careful not to project the values of your society on to her. She published and had definite views. These superficially point towards emancipation and free thought, yet her texts have no sense of the function of society to protect its weak. The idea of state benevolence could not be developed in her mindset. That would come later. Her locations were the meeting places of Georgian free thought but after some years she moved to an isolated house in the Lake District. Harriet often astounded me with her views, yet my reactive position allows her precise propositions to resonate across the century. We are dealing with mental excursions that point towards the development of self-help societies – whatever they might be. Think of the connection between Malthus and Robert McNamara. I am the link, at least I am for one evening only. Leading towards sites for freethinking that have been and will be. With your new multiple moralities and your desire to operate in the gaps maybe it will be hard to rationalise my position. When considering the link between Malthus and McNamara it is necessary to digress into McNamara's own narrative. Robert McNamara, former head of Ford, Secretary of Defense under Kennedy and consultant on population growth in the late 1960s. He brought freethinking business practice to bear on the issue of perceived population explosion, sorting things out, and having a conscience. The McNamara viewpoint is novelistic so let us enter that tunnel system."

Words spoken in an American accent. But the person talking is an elderly Englishman. "If I understand what is being said, then I would suggest that the central argument is held in place by an understanding of the way in which analysis of activity affects activity. In fact, in time it might be possible to get lost between the two. Reaching towards a point where it is impossible to do anything much other than flit between doing something and watching what takes place. But that sounds a bit depressing or even negative. So maybe it would be better to try and put a positive gloss on all this movement. If you do 'it' and watch 'it' at the same time, if analysis and action become truly reflexive then maybe that helps people to understand, or at least demonstrate that they are beginning to come to terms with the peculiar temporary nature of their condition." Bob makes a mental note of his contribution.

CHAPTER SIX
GRAPE STREET WINE BAR

Erasmus walks straight into the bar. Downstairs into a cramped basement space. He orders a glass of red wine and takes a seat in the corner of the room.

For the purposes of this guide to a London that you may visit, we will be replaying a fiction set in tunnels that are supposed to exist under the White House and transferring it to the tunnels that now exist under Centre Point. They are both new systems for Erasmus. Centre Point, that symbolic, hard to access building is currently a base for the Confederation of British Industries. But in its tunnels some debate takes place. It is a place for the new generation of freethinkers. I know what McNamara would say.

Chunking up ideas. Rather than attempting to look at each one with precise, pedantic care. In this way control may be assumed over segments of an argument. The pieces can be incorporated into larger concepts in order to proceed without having to go back to the beginning each time. This enables the processing of statistics to go ahead. Projection is possible and profits generated. Erasmus likes chunking. Looped ideas are hard to discuss. If he consid ered such questions with any less care, he might as well just go home and take responsibility for his guests.

Harriet has nearly heard enough. "I think we all agree, that even with the absence of our host, we all seek a degree of understanding. That we would be prepared to make an effort to communicate. But understanding, as sought by true freethinkers, feeds the development of individual arguments. A set of hyper-individuals, drawn together in a consideration of detail. Each separate idea reflecting off the other until interchange goes beyond straightforward rationalisation."

But within the development of arguments during an evening such as this, some characters are eclipsed. It would, in fact, be true to say that ideas about pure dialogue are just that— pure ideas. But if Murry, Harriet or even absent Erasmus were to object to a fundamental portion of debate how would they find space in which to express this dissatisfaction? Further to this, it seems as if the guests have each developed quite liquid types of exchange. Listening sometimes, but continuing regardless most of the time. I'm sure that they all realise that they are engaged in varied forms of moral outrage, but have no tools with which to dismantle that potential due to the fact that there is a collective sense that at some point, if they continue as they are, moral outrage itself will become debased and hard to pin down.

So back to the tunnels under Centre Point. And it's McNamara's own story.

"If you want to fight then you go underground, whether you're on the inside of things or on the outside. I don't know who told me first. Sometimes it feels like I always knew about them. Every great castle has secret passages. Routes and conduits for information and escape. The new places, the twentieth-century palaces have them too. Think about it; all the big military wings have always been located underground. Underground, a metaphor and the literal state of things. But it came as a surprise to find out about the tunnels under the White House. I don't know why it should have been a surprise. It makes perfect sense. The White House is just a big place where power is located. A big place, but big like a Tokyo department store. Small on top with a labyrinth below. People use the tunnels. They're a means of escape and arrival but also a place to be." There is a strong feeling among the other guests that this is just the beginning of a much longer story.

CHAPTER SEVEN
THE TUNNELS UNDER CENTRE POINT

Under Centre Point there's a snooker hall and some public lavatories. Erasmus has finally arrived, but not at the dinner. He prefers to spend his time in a place that's open all night. Standing here illuminated by the soft flicker of fluorescent lights, Erasmus remembers a story. What a surprise, he is caught in a reverie. His thoughts move to another tunnel, a tunnel in his future but in our past. A narrative that includes one of the dinner guests. As before, this is really McNamara's story, part of it at least. But no one is clear whose turn it is to tell the tale. At least we know who is listening.

"Present are Robert McNamara, Secretary of Defense, and Herman Kahn of the RAND INSTITUTE. It is dark, Kahn carries a flashlight. McNamara is prematurely balding. He wears glasses. His hair is dark and his eyes precise. Kahn is half a step behind him, always looking for a way in. McNamara stops dead. 'There's a gap between his image and the historical reality. Despite everything it's possible to rework a situation. That's why his popularity at home and abroad remained at super-high levels, even though we are talking about a really short period of time.'" Kahn, shorter and...

There is more later.

The dream-state is interrupted and we are back in Great Marlborough Street. A sentence is spoken, but no one is quite sure who said it.

"Procedure and analysis are continually being re-defined and therefore people have begun to look for certainty." Harriet waits for his reply.

"As I continue on my way." (It must be Erasmus, attempting to communicate from the tunnel) "No that's too strong, it implies that there is some clear trajectory. As I stand and fail to arrive. Yes. Maybe your sense of certainty about the formation of society will be replaced by a set of multiple certainties. In fact even that earlier certainty was always underscored by fear. But maybe it will be possible to create a constantly mobile moral construction and use that to counter the equally rapid shifts (in physical terms) that we are bound to encounter. Possibly we will be able to enforce a flexible moral condition upon a number of activities as well. Some people will speak about the end of utopias, but I doubt if a time of truly rapid interchange will ever be possible." Erasmus is smiling.

"As a way to adjust to the complicated material changes that will inevitably take place, it might be necessary to identify the gaps between these alterations. If the gaps are identified then it could be said that stop and start points will reveal themselves. Points of entry towards temporary solutions and points of exit away from temporary crisis. The form of flexible morality that I alluded to earlier will not close things down, on the contrary, if we play the right games then such a flexible position will lead to increased potential for irresponsibility and a new, dynamic form of debate. This is really a logical continuation of a number of ideas. It could be the case that any attempt to apply moral and ethical rules in isolation is and has always been impossible. Therefore it is necessary to look for signposts. A search for social theories in relation to a freethinking vision will only lead to clumsiness. Yet that process has already begun. As we reach the middle of this important night, ways forward will become the goal. Even if there is a general recognition of the need to find rapidly flickering multiple positions, people will still want to make judgements. They might even want to encourage a certain degree of censorship in order to back up those little morals. But this is where the problem starts. How are we going to find a way to examine a social structure without the old moral hierarchies? We are all going to find liquid censorship difficult. It will be a question of looking for and encouraging a sense of self-censorship. A degree of pressure on the individual that will inevitably cause problems. It depends whether you are involved in established religion or not."

Erasmus is not entirely happy. "If I stood up and shouted at you I would not be ignored. Yet it might be more interesting if I merely expressed my arguments with clarity and calmness. I would attract a different kind of attention. But I suggest that the degree of engagement would be diminished. I'm sure you would be familiar with the way in which I was behaving. There might be a time when I appeared to be sharing a number of sober points but was in fact formulating carefully calculated single statements that bore no relationship to each other. Therefore you could say that the structure of our fractured evening permits some great intelligence and some quite extraordinary stupidity. Some of the guests who await me are capable of both extremes at once. I cannot ignore them but I also do not really appreciate the prospect of returning home to face them just yet. It would be forgivable if everyone began to distance themselves from my analysis of avoidance. But I think everyone has been waiting around long enough for us to skip past such an acute reflection upon manners and move directly to thinking about what must be taking place in my home. Have I forgotten or am I involved in a deliberate absence?"

There will be a point after this Georgian interlude when thinkers will begin to focus upon specific manifestations of behaviour and language rather than making generalised comments that could be said to embrace an attitude connected to modern utopias that are as stale as the utopias they replaced. Focus is placed upon people in a way that is different to Erasmus's concentration or belief in the individual as a way through a particular set of problems. Thinking at that point evades him. Inconsistent, irrational and rooted in the varied manifestations of a particular person.

The freethinker as an insider rather than an outsider. Social examination as a science might grab him. That old outsider idea will last a long time, but maybe there will be a point when it appears as if the symbolic potential will merely be a hollow shell. For there is a big difference between choosing to operate outside certain codes that define our society and being forced to operate outside. This does not involve any conspiracy theory, it is merely the due process of the libertarian opium-addled mind of Erasmus. Everything will appear in real time for a while. Yet this existential solution can have no real lasting validity. There will be humour. Much more is possible at dinners such as this. Maybe there is some pointed comedy that binds those people who still wait for their host together. But it is so over-stated and under-presented that it is impossible for Erasmus to pin it down. He is too worried. For he has a younger brother. A man with a stomach that will cause him great distress. But for now let's just reflect on the things people say and do. Some of the connections that may take place on an evening such as this but will go unsaid. There's a time slip that gains access through a ventilation shaft in the kitchen. Bang an offcut of plywood over the hole and you would lose everything.

CHAPTER EIGHT
THE POSTER STUDIO

The Poster Studio is a centre for possible action. But to truly get involved there has to be an understanding of the potential of an occupation of time as much as space. Erasmus has walked a short distance from the subway under Centre Point. He stands at the entrance to a large Georgian building while people rush past. It's a familiar place but seems to have aged rapidly since he last came across it. Banging on the door. He looks tired. It takes a lot of effort to remain engaged in a time slip.

Back under the White House, McNamara's story continues. "… stouter always looking distracted. Concentrating hard on the job. Feeling for a way in to McNamara's approaches around the subject. Always more direct. Less precise but more direct. This time he is off track, out of the line of the non-spoken conversation that has led them into the tunnel system. 'Uh?,' Kahn stands, turning to McNamara. 'There's a contradiction here.' His eyes are milky in the fluorescent light. McNamara stops. Adjusts his glasses and looks right past Kahn straight back down the tunnel. 'Concentrate Herman, we're right underneath this time. The question of how to reposition is central to all this.' Kahn shifts. A bulky ill-defined presence in the gloom. He's been had. Swerving from the facts. Herman believes it can all be worked out. 'But the figures make everything seem so clear.' McNamara pulls back. Time for some statistics to make things plain or loaded. 'He reached a high of 83 per cent approval in the Gallup Polls after the Bay of Pigs and stayed within the sixtieth and seventieth percentiles right through this year.' Kahn's eyes focus, his body straightens, when he brings his full attention to bear on a McNamara wisdom the change in his demeanour always throws the other man. 'Nobody says percentiles Bob, nobody—not yet.'"

Hot and cold. Elsie has something. A graspable way to characterise different modes of communication. Some ways to pass information are hotter than others. It's not something she has ever written down. But Erasmus knows the full theory. She'll pass it on to her son. Don't worry. In the meantime there are rumours that she will continue beating him with a razor strop until he remembers all the longest words.

(*This time we are outside the White House. Two other characters are about to appear.*)

"Washington in the early 1960s. The place with everything and nothing. Not a place without hope, yet. Where the centre and the periphery are in close partnership. And tunnels, those tunnels, underscoring everything. The place to be. But now we are in a motel. Next to the highway the rooms are functional. A television in the corner of one. A bed with nylon sheets. A sateen cover is rucked while a half quart of whisky sits on the brown table top. It's not as bad as it sounds, just there and basic. A window overlooks the car lot. It is covered with net and fancied drapes. The women are not quite fully dressed. In the bathroom Fiddle is peering. The mirror is still misted. 'Americans tend to equate good looks with intelligence, sensitivity, sincerity …'

"Faddle is her friend, they are easy together. Easy in a way that McNamara and Kahn can never attain. She likes to finish the sentences of her friend: 'Self-confidence, independence, poise, competence and…' The two women look over their shoulders. One is still peering in the mirror, the other checking the door. There is silence for a second and a barely perceptible scratching noise. A spark transfers from one to the other. They think hard and lose their comfort."

Erasmus has some favourite subjects. Freethinking, freeloading, freebasing, freefalling. Ways to heighten a loss of responsibility. At Erasmus's starting point it's the only way to move into the future. But it will lead nowhere. As far as he is concerned any embryonic sense of society is being wrenched from the church and rebuilt by a secular structure. One that will require constant attack.

"I'll admit that people have tried this before. Attempts have been made to enter the realm of the unconscious. Not subconscious, but truly opiated near-sleep. There's little point in viewing this collection of people as a group. Although Erasmus denies that he is interested in leading such a group, were it to exist, I feel that he would be the natural head." Harriet is confident in her ideas.

Opium taken regularly. Never smoked, like a peasant or an addict, but prescribed and eaten in pastille form. Insomnia as a result of this medication.

CHAPTER NINE

It's the middle of the night. Imagine the complete loss of necessity for sleep. Wandering back from The Poster Studio. A special offer. The opportunity to watch people. Right on the north-west corner of the crossroads. The junction of Oxford Street and Tottenham Court Road.

No one is talking but back in the tunnel Kahn is still thinking. He has snapped out of the Bob-induced circumnavigation of the facts. He wants to work things out for a minute. Get an overview of the situation. The only way to do this is to talk. Talking is easy with Bob at times like this. Here, in the tunnel, where you can be anywhere but underground.

"'Good character Bob.' Something clicks. Kahn feels light. At moments like this everything becomes clearer, not everything that he has been attending to but everything about the location of power. The tunnel, acting like a feeder system or a neuro-network, mirroring his unease. The feeling of being flung back through the entire network is exhilarating and devastating."

Murry is not convinced. "I can see your reasoning, I think. Maybe it is beginning to happen. It's possibly tonight that Erasmus becomes the ultimate parallel leader. But there's some irony in this. He is so close to a symbolic core of achievement. This happens with every truly engaged parallel excursion. Certain theoretical structures that have and will emerge could help us to navigate such a proposition. Anything with large doses of romanticism, Marxism and a simple pleasure in toying with everyday objects. At some point, as a follow-up to what has been said, this group may realise that relatively straightforward transformations are worth observing. Whether or not they are worth mimicking and then repeating is another question. But merely copying the things that they see tonight may also have some power. What really interests me is an idea connected to refusing any clear-cut position regardless of the circumstances. So that there may be a person or collection of people who always refuse and always indicate their recognition of a collapse of society that depends on an ability to read detail, undermining any serious progression through extreme personal engagement, multiple morality and autobiography. This isn't exactly humour but it is certainly a rejection of gravity. None of the people here tonight could accept laziness, insolence, humour and egomania as codes to live by, but they will. Because the obvious result of what is taking place remains entirely connected to the fact that one might be able to recognise how varied the Georgian position will become. Asking questions, contradicting each other. After fear comes vagueness and a desire to start again, it is inevitable that no more consensus will be possible. It's everyone against everyone from now on."

Erasmus can't let that go without a reply. "The whole idea that I am isolated and lost will be talked about at great length. But if my position is not unique why on earth would it be interesting to talk about it? And if I chose to leave nothing behind, will that make my thoughts any less valuable? I will speak through other people."

CHAPTER TEN
RICHARD WOLFF'S PLACE

Having walked west down Oxford Street, it appears as if Erasmus is heading home. Certainly he is wearily awaited. But in Soho there is a building that requires investigation. A place where still images are captured in a dirty, run-down location. A site for the collation of desires. Richard Wolff. Sitting in his room. Pulling focus and moving a large articulated tripod while carefully rebuilding another narrative.

Erasmus speaks. "Maybe it is time to reflect upon the vague substance of my position in relation to the others. You have to understand the legacy of a non-conformist family. My grandfather and father were closely connected to the growth of production technologies as you know them. And as a result they also contributed to the evolution of theories around such activity. They were friends with those people who attempted to refine the methods of profit maximisation and they also engaged in embryonic forms of capitalist speculation. Yet at that point they were operating with little sense of the effect of their projections. They tried hard to peer into the very near future. There was a little understanding and a great degree of goodwill but all that was tied up with a level of pragmatic theorising that could not really foresee its effects. It seems now as if their investigations of production would inevitably lead them to increased wealth. But it couldn't be predicted in advance. And it was the realisation of the importance of prediction that helped them to maximise their profits. The difference is the relationship between land and wealth compared to industry and wealth. Moving from a position where land generates money to a speculative strategy.

"The people who came just before me had great hopes and felt close to adventure. In spirit their approach appears to have been risk-based, but in reality they couldn't lose. Their distrust of the establishment was real enough but not sustainable in the long run, it was a critique from within, and because of this it was reactive rather than oppositional. A by-product was the creation of self-awareness on the part of the displaced people they employed. It was not grounded in a set of locked humanist principles. Even though you may think that it was. There's no reason to believe that the relative positions people held would not remain fixed. In light of this thinking they could proceed unencumbered by a belief in progress while relying on it at the same time. They could only begin to think in terms of futurology. And they could only just begin the process of looking forward. Nothing could cloud a vision of the potential of production."

But Erasmus has a solution too:
"Flickering between one mode of behaviour and another will suffice. This could be as simple as the choice of what to wear. One way of expanding a set of ideas. Acting like an eccentric while everyone else attempts to predict their growth. There are always groups of people who float between varied activities. They have been fetishised into significance so many times that I have become weary attempting to keep count. As a Georgian I do not have much time. A more profound way of looking at things is inevitable. A social science, a Marxist science. That will come later, and in the meantime my thinking will be appropriated by conservative people. But at least I am starting to realise that my position is not passive. Everything is changing. Even my brother recognises this. Once the process has begun it may not be stopped. There's a whole mess of inconsistency, irrationality and personality."

Everyone can hear him now. And Elsie is not alone in her determination to convince him of impending tragedy.

"Any developed dialogue will exhibit a level of complexity. This might ensure that debate, as such, may not receive much attention. And rhetoric will be seen as a solution. But a concentration upon the structure of this evening's discussion alone may not be sufficient to explain the actions of the main protagonists or the social shifts that they are concerned with. The recognition that we are faced with complexity merely proves that one impenetrable structure tends to be replaced by another. Some Georgian libertarian free-marketeers relied upon diverse strategies. Collecting positions from varied sources. Yet most of the time this behaviour was symbolic rather than actual.

"Is it possible to draw parallels across to a postmodern condition? Probably not. A lot of this is dependent on your perception of the key starting points of modernism as an identifiable period. Of course there is an element of detail and attention to a-moralistic positions that mirror attempts to transcend abstraction and metaphorical references to the failure of utopias. Making films and playing games. There are artificial constructs here which deserve attention. There may be no film or television culture for a Georgian but soon we'll have the Regent Street Polytechnic. Little in the way of dogmatic ideology holds back or frees our participants. There are varied positions adopted, lost and regained. All of this is framed within a set of dynamically contradictory statements."

Fermat's last theorem worked out in the margin or on a napkin. Just one of the activities taking place in a small dining room. The image of the participants is beginning to fade as they become engaged in things that are common to us all. As soon as they can recognise shared agendas, their reason to wait will collapse.

Erasmus is reaching a series of conclusions. He's never been this articulate before. "The view used to be held that the circumstances people found themselves in were connected to a set of higher regulations. The importance of the period that I have lived through is the realisation that this set of static positions could be challenged precisely because it was so fixed. It could be challenged because however hard you tried to break the conceptual system down, it had been sustained for such a long period of time that it appeared to be unassailable. And because of this it was a brittle construct. But from this evening onwards we are considering an industrial revolutionary period that set up the re-moralised neo-Christian model of apparently democratic free-marketeering that is yet to be transcended. The clumsy state utopias of your century (the twentieth?) were a last gasp. Harking back to an earlier period when people supposedly knew where they stood. These were historical aberrations with disastrous consequences. A desire for certainty in a context of an unstoppable shift towards classic laissez-faire behaviour as you may or may not know it. The deconstruction of moralities and linguistic game playing that reframes all the terms that we were supposed to have been familiar with."

CHAPTER ELEVEN
LONDON UNIVERSITY

Disguised as the British Museum. In fact, University College would be a more accurate choice. It reminds Masaru of a story he once heard from his host and best friend, one day, years ago.

Erasmus: "Why did the Georgian freethinker take opium?"
Harriet: "Because of a complex set of social and economic factors."

Erasmus: "The desire to see into the near future and to predict trends was not something that existed in a precise, effective form until people began to project aboutproduction. But then I am trapped into saying this by the fact that my identity rides across such a relatively lengthy period of time. I now understand that the desire to predict the near future changes the future. Trying to think about the near future produced massive wealth for a small group, nothing new in that, the difference was in the way that the money was realised. They had not thought that these attempts would naturally change the course of events. Some people sitting around near Birmingham considering growth and potential. And increased wealth was complemented by a rise in fear of its producers. Today is the day that the mob become the workers."

Unbelievable. Erasmus is hooked. He's walked in the opposite direction, away from his own house. Gone right back for one last look at the electronic goods on offer. If only he realised he was standing outside a normal hi-fi shop in Tottenham Court Road.

McNamara wants to leave, he's becoming bored of the repetition and the embarrassment of witnessing a person grappling with ideas with which he is already over-familiar. He better say something to try a draw the evening to a close.

"The workers. A set that did not exist for our host. A group of people that would need definition. Pulling themselves up by their bootstraps, as Harriet used to say. They should be encouraged. They have been defined and replaced within the scope of this guide. The classic fear of the increasing education of the workers. A Malthusian fear of population explosion. These anxieties were not carefully constructed. Pulling yourself up rather than over-producing. But pulling up collectively. The rise of organisation. The terminology did not exist. It is fading in and out of consciousness. It did not happen at the beginning and it's being talked out of existence in the end. Free thought, individuality, the freedom to be alone. Fear that was no longer fear because the idea had no sustainable construction. There have been riots and there have been mobs. But the rise of a set of people who would then be able to define themselves caused a number of problems. It was impossible for the people Erasmus came into contact with in his youth to attempt to define themselves because they would have no self-image until later. It was not possible to fear an educated working population that had only just been theorised into existence."

A reply is necessary. "So much of what is taking place is ordinary. But can we really define a sense of the everyday that has any significant continuity? For although we are witnessing the evolution of conditions that will permit mass production, we are as yet incapable of analysing the results. Our powers of prediction do not allow us to read behaviour through objects alone. Yet maybe it is possible to work through the increasing diversification of layered cultural expression, and in this way to work out what has taken place. And to predict the production of things that may be allowed to act as modified icons in order to back up these ways of behaving. Advertising and promotional techniques may permit the development and acceptance of production surplus. Individuality dominates debate at this point due to the fact that everything points towards endless possibility. It is all very well to open up new trading opportunities, but only with some idea of the possible consequences of such actions. The idea of failure that is built into early Christian moral structures could well survive. But spaces left between desire and commodity will provide a peculiar situation—an extreme expression of loss. Competition is our only manifesto but it is a way of thinking that can only exist when there is no real competition."

It seems quite clear that Erasmus is not going to make it home in time to meet his guests. What are the consequences of this absence? Well, just think of how much clearer the debate might have been if they had all been sitting together in the same room. And as a guide it could be said that there is a lack of any specific indications of where to go and how to get there. As implied by Erasmus at the outset, this was never going to be easy or clear. As time passes, and the night approaches day the mob are about to wake to a new beginning. They will be given the tools with which to attack the structures that hold them down. It will take some time, that is certain, yet quite soon, sooner than Erasmus dare imagine, there will be a whole new set of discursive positions open to them and closed to him. And as soon as that potential is realised it will metamorphose and we will witness another set of new beginnings.

At this point we can only be sure of one thing. Erasmus's brother will find out a great deal in his world tour. And these discoveries will terrify him into inactivity. Late in the day he will publish. There's one last chance. A return once more to the small, comfortable dining room in Great Marlborough Street, to see if anything can be salvaged from a debate about debate.

CHAPTER TWELVE
GO HOME

Dumping goods on other markets. A technique employed to ensure the corruption of that longed-for fantasy of free trade and exchange. It has been a recurring sub-text. A matter of great concern to all the people here. Well, maybe not for Murry, but even he is starting to believe that he is part of this free-market dynamic. After all, it is people like him who will defend it most rigorously, even while hiding behind a protectionist position that would stun Erasmus, if he were to truly understand it.

The white table cloth is stained. Some of the guests have even made notes directly onto its surface. It seems as if this house has no note paper. There is a rumour that later in life, or was it earlier, Erasmus wrote some poetry. This may be true, but he certainly wasn't writing much at the time of this meal. Near the beginning of the supper there had been a search for paper and pens at a point when Masaru felt it necessary to explain the u-shaped pricing curve. Despite Elise's thorough search through the house not a single scrap of paper or any writing implements could be found. Fortunately Bob had a pen, so they began to work straight onto the table cloth. Elsie didn't approve, Harriet loved the idea, McNamara thought it a practical solution, Masaru was no longer paying attention and Murry didn't care either way.

And we can see them all sitting there. The question of whether or not they have eaten anything is irrelevant to the narrative. Erasmus is still trying to communicate.

"Yes, yes." Erasmus is warming up, and so late in the day. "Guilds, apprentices and societies. But not the workers. An optimism prevailed and it is one that still exists for me. A belief in development—that people stuck in a specific social crisis will rise above it. A relative growth, based on freethinking and lack of overwhelming control. I enjoy hearing your people harking back to a time before their confused attempts at social responsibility. We believed that people would help themselves but we could not imagine how they would do it. The ideas shifted across the Atlantic and the Channel. We could not imagine them using our terminology. The development of a language that can deal with the concept of communication. Something to be subjected to and something to involve yourself in. The adjustment of Elysian utopias into materialist utopias. The variability and mutability of non-conformist theory. A degree of pragmatism. And we had it all. Ecology. Biology. Technology and a lump of opium dissolved. Toying with another salmon supper."

Masaru is starting to understand something. The others give him permission to reply. "Under consideration, as before, is the role of opium-eating Georgian freethinkers and the particular positions they adopted. In turn the contextualising complex that evolves as a direct result of critical dementia and debating inertia have been addressed, followed by a theoretical model for behavioural possibilities in light of the clichés that have been exposed through the discussion of other matters."

Erasmus is remembering his past at last. "I studied anatomy and got all of the horrible jobs. I had to cut up and clear up the bodies. But that is a story that remains unparalleled. There is a satisfying aspect to this development of overall control. The desire for perpetual revolution continually reframed by one figurehead. The initiation of what turned out to be perpetual stasis disguised in the form of cycles of crisis. All of this underscored by the dominance of one group over another. My brother will imply that these groups are replaceable. But the issue that is familiar to me is the continual urge to re-invigorate a population. And is this terrifying? I think it is. And the fear of freedom to move and to comment holds people back. At times it feels as if there is a cumulative effect. Something akin to removing elements from a precarious pile of objects. It is possible to carefully take away any number of supports until, with little warning for those who pay no attention, the whole structure collapses. In my earlier time, we would have to picture this series of events the other way round."

Erasmus realises he is not being very clear: "Think of it like viewing one of your films in reverse. The basic framework is in a state of comfortable repose on the ground. Scattered. Remember, this is only a metaphor. A group is considering the debris. Suddenly the tower of disparate parts will shoot up. Unsteady. Rocking to and fro. Within a short time elements are added. Creating increasing stability. The important thing for me to do is see this process in reverse and forwards simultaneously in order to comprehend completely the doubled contradictory possibilities of what is about to come. Many only see the removal of elements towards imminent collapse. Others see only addition. There are groups who see this process as inevitable, some feel that it can be affected. It is only the brief moment in time before either the forward or reverse movement that truly interests me. A last opportunity for classical utopianism in the face of a series of dynamic shifts that will lead to multiple aspirations rather than visionary hierarchies."

Ibuka takes no notice. The line of communication is breaking down, but he's still got one or two things to say. "A consideration of the minimal spatial unit, the gap or even the time slip. Some examples."

These are clearly the kinds of issues that he is interested to examine, but for the moment there is no real engagement with what he is saying.

This whole question is linked to notions of permission. It is important to consider ideas of institutionalised compromise and the extent to which practitioners feel that they can acknowledge failure. The sub-text is that there is no fundamental difference between various mediators of time, the people who control how it is used, and analysts of the current position of society. Further to this I propose that an intellectual framework exists in order to come to terms with the perceived contradictions that are thrown up by the possession of control over the way in which time passes and analysis of how it is controlled. If not, why are there so many books and films that centre of the idea of a time slip of one sort or another? It remains appealing. Such excursions help to define place and potential, and as such need to be taken seriously.

If only we were all there. The heavy oak furniture is as hard to date as anything. The soft yellow glow of the lights flashing off the glassware. Silver cutlery, blackened and shiny in equal measure. A group of people. A set of faces across a table. An embarrassing time for everyone.

Harriet has something to say.

"The critical language employed by freethinkers is, for the most part, shared. This particular form of coming together and blurring of activities will help to define class and struggle. Since the early eighteenth century there has been no fundamental difference between the languages used to discuss the most interesting freethinking and the way in which the most conventional activities were talked about. It could be said that there was a inevitability about a meeting like this."

It's time to refill the glasses.

Elsie interrupts.

"I think you will find that there is only a difference in self-perception on the part of the practitioners. Even the formal quality of the two modes of thinking is often shared. In order to demonstrate this it is important to understand two main strands of my work that involve and illustrate the blurring that I am talking about. If you try and imagine the opposite of freethinking, it might suffice for this one example to start a consideration of careful, responsible social management. And if you proceed to think about these two apparent extremes it becomes clear that there are other spaces thrown up by these two areas that can be usefully occupied. This is because when dealing with the most interesting freethinking and the most effective social planning we should not only consider division and definition but recognise that the most effective alternatives to these structures exist in the gaps allowed by the rest of society.

This is not restricted to social concepts but refers to all activities that shape and frame the spaces where we live, work, think and play."

McNamara's heard enough. Not interested in relativism. How can anyone be surprised that Harriet has considered a move to the country and an end to her ridiculous pamphleteering.

"I know that you are desperate to introduce religious allusions. And that you are really only constructing 'cathedrals to debate'."

Who would have thought such an outburst would come from him.

"It affords me the first occasion to use the word 'God' in a semi-serious discussion."

Erasmus is starting to feel sick. He must find a place to rest. He can't remember where he is any longer. There are no clear signposts or recognisable landmarks.

McNamara is not finished yet.
"As a result, in such elevated company it gives me great pleasure to talk about failure and compromise. When I talk of compromise I mean the western form of the idea of historically determined self-image. People in the past who worked for society through organised Christian religion always failed even if they became materially rich. That failure was built into the structures of humility. Any activity could be interpreted as a tribute to God."

This is not what Erasmus had hoped for. If only he could find his way back towards his own home. He stumbles from Tottenham Court Road towards Soho. Making his way across the square. Into Dean Street and across towards Wardour Street. He's back near Richard Wolff's place. But he realises for the first time that the building is empty. He has completely failed to enter any of the places he has visited. He should have checked each one. They will all be functioning later, but he doesn't know that yet.

McNamara continues, but no one is really listening anymore.

"Rather than being more compromised it could be argued that traditionally the administrator or organiser has not been able to fail enough. Not coy about constructing a model for society, because on one level it worked. As with a building, it worked as long as it stood and did not fall over. This functionality exists before you get to any discussion of a theoretical structure's real content. Sure, traditional free thought has a structural set of rules but they are not necessarily implicit in the final effect until you get towards a discussion of twentieth-century social democratic state control."

At the end there is bound to be some music. And of all the guests tonight it is Murry who could provide it. Neither the Canadian or the English woman appear to be with us any more. He's left it too late, but Murry is engaged. Try and imagine a suitable score to go along with his final statement.

"Since the decline of established western religions people have begun to consider thinkers in a radically different way. The shield of institutionalised failure has become a linguistic conceit. For the first time in the western world the freethinker is no longer viewed as compromised. The idea has instead been displaced on to the social planner. All of this underscored by an acknowledgement of humanism, existential angst and now multiple referencing combined with layered neo-morality."

Erasmus is never going to make it. Already the guests are fading. It would only be right to give him the last words, but I think everyone would doubt his ability to use them correctly. Any order will do. As he staggers towards Berwick Street, nearly home. Later than ever. There will be no revolution now. No chance of a firm reversal of the situation as we know it. He must become resolved to the fact that from now on there will only be decline. His ideas, if you can call them that, will be appropriated by the Right and the Left in order to maintain things as they are. A way to provide a shaky reasoning for markets and growth and a formula with which to attack that structure.

So, as he wanders, breathless, Erasmus speaks once more. He is starting to realise what he has missed. The chance for a guide to London written across time and the possibility of lasting change.

"The thinker remains compromised, as before, but is now caught within a web of social constructions rather than precise goals. Since the development of leisure, people have spoken of the best ideas as 'free' and 'uncompromised' or even 'true'. All these phrases are used to try and regain a 'spiritual' dimension that never actually existed. Although they were phrases used historically, in the past they tended to refer to the formal properties of an idea not its potential. As a result the thinker remains fetishised by other people. In this case, by organisers, administrators and technologists. The best freethinkers are interested in the various manifestations of complex social construction. Bureaucracy is perfectly centred in this debate and is therefore closer in spirit to pure concepts at this moment than in any other time since the relatively recent development of the professionalisation of administration. There's a difference between an administrator and a clerk. There will be a gulf between planning and practise. Use it."

And Murry sits back in his chair. It's nearly five o'clock in the morning. Always the last to leave. (He's probably worried about his percentage.) Still no sign of Erasmus. And the others have melted away. Murry did not notice them leave. He snuffs out a candle and makes his way downstairs. If you think of the empty room, so recently vacated, then it might be possible to imagine the sound of a key in the door. The incompleteness of Fermat's Solution fades on the napkin. And heavy footsteps approach up the stairs.

IBUKA!

A book based on ERASMUS IS LATE. This text was published slightly ahead of the book it refers to. As with McNAMARA, the book is a work that was the central component of an exhibition. Where McNAMARA used a cartoon as a form to carry a narrative, IBUKA! was conceived as an instruction for how it might be possible to produce a popular musical based on the book ERASMUS IS LATE. In both cases, popular art forms are used to carry complex ideas. IBUKA! is Masaru Ibuka, the co-founder of Sony. It is in this text that we find some clear description of the characters in its source book ERASMUS IS LATE and some further developments of the ideas within it.

IBUKA! A musical in three acts based on the book
ERASMUS IS LATE

PREFACE
The characters in the book are derived from an adaptation
of ERASMUS IS LATE. So a stage setting must be visualised
and various possibilities explored. IBUKA! is a musical
entertainment that deals with the roots of our current
situation and the embryonic status of socialism and western
European capitalism at the beginning of the nineteenth
century. It's a song and dance spectacular, despite the fact
that none of the words or music have been written as yet.

PART 1
SETTING

IBUKA! is at its heart a layered musical. It should appear as
if various locations and actions can be presented
simultaneously. IBUKA! should be entertaining, with
memorable songs and powerful, easily remembered lyrics.
The basic treatment of the set is all that requires outlining.
The chosen space should be brightly painted, using a wide
range of colours. The result should be overwhelming and
pleasing in equal measure. Various props are described in
this text. These may be fully developed at a later point. It is
important, however, to indicate the presence of a table at
the heart of this musical. It should be as large as possible,
heavy and constructed with little fuss, ornament or detailing.
Strong lighting is necessary in order to fully appreciate the
dramatic possibilities outlined later on. It is a good idea, at
this stage, for potential promoters of this musical to consider
listening to the widely available Warner Brothers' CD of Carl
Stalling compositions. He wrote scores for Warner Brothers'
cartoons in the 1940s and 1950s.

PART 2
CHARACTERS

Various characters are present and it is necessary to indicate something of their appearance and their personality traits. Interpretation will be left to anyone who stages the musical and the people who take part in its performance. The central character is Erasmus. He should be played by a mature man with a good, strong, but rather high-pitched singing voice. If this is not possible he should at least be capable of a wide range of vocal styles. At all times Erasmus should be wearing the following clothes: a black tophat. This should be in good condition yet may be dusty or slightly dirty. Black trousers, high cut and narrow in the leg. No underwear. A dirty white shirt and cravat. A woollen waistcoat is necessary because Erasmus spends the duration of the musical wandering around the streets of London. Heavy black boots are worn for the same reason. In his pocket Erasmus always carries a small silver box. Inside this container are his opium pastilles. These will appear frequently during the musical. Silk socks are one of his favourite things. And a copy of the book ERASMUS IS LATE is frequently visible, poking out of his jacket pocket.

Erasmus, like all the other characters, has very specific moods. He appears slightly bilious at all times, as if he has heartburn, a mild stomach ulcer or just indigestion. On top of this he is clearly out of it. Already under the influence of a heavy narcotic but never drunk. He can speak and sing clearly but his manner on stage indicates some near-complete inebriation. He meanders around. Clearly wise but lacking in direction. Despite all these things he remains lucid, if rather dreamy. This is a time for reflection and a peculiar form of non-action for Erasmus and his portrayal should indicate this from the outset. He will become increasingly disturbed as the musical develops.

Harriet Martineau is his best friend. Erasmus and Harriet have a platonic yet extremely close relationship. She is wearing a large hat. The design is rather eccentric and the crown of the hat is trimmed heavily with lace. A long dress allows only fleeting glimpses of black boots, laced high. A small purse is either in her hand or by her side on the table top at all times. She wears white gloves and carries a number of paperback pamphlets in her hands. A large brooch is pinned to her dress. She likes to carry a stick or cane but seems not to need it in order to move around. A bottle of smelling salts is a necessary accompaniment to the pamphlets and allows rapid revival of people who have read the contents of her radical libertarian booklets. Her character is clear-cut. Harriet is determined, always taking a position which indicates that everything is read in relation to everything else. Throughout this musical she remains focused, yet there are many times when she contradicts herself.

Masaru Ibuka does not say much. He likes his Walkman. After all, it was his idea. He also carries a large number of pens. Apart from that, his dress code fits with late-twentieth-century business practices. A charcoal grey suit and a fresh white shirt. He likes to wear boxer shorts under his suit, shiny black shoes on his feet and is never seen without a black tie. His tie is sometimes loosened and at other times tucked into his shirt, but it never comes off, even on the hottest days. In order to concentrate, especially when making notes or working out calculations, Masaru often carries a green printer's visor. And occasionally will take a printed circuit board from his pocket at moments of boredom or disengagement. This happens very rarely, however, because most of the time he concentrates hard on what is being said, speculating wildly on the potential of a meeting like this. He is always inventive, experimental yet respectful. In fact it is quite clear that Masaru Ibuka is a good dinner guest, if only because he is a good listener.

Robert McNamara has recently become a more familiar character. At the time when I wrote the original version of McNAMARA in 1992 it was often necessary to explain who he was. Now people have a much clearer picture. For the purposes of this exhibition he is clean-cut and wears glasses. McNamara prefers a dark blue suit and a blue and white striped shirt combined with a red tie. His shoes are black and extremely clean. He is rarely seen without his briefcase. From this slim leather bag he produces a large number of important looking buff folders full of various papers, agreements, accords and proposals. It would be good to say that he has an assistant, but there is no place for one in this scenario. This is not normal and it makes him feel uneasy. McNamara doesn't travel alone. For some reason that is hard to explain he also carries a torch. And more predictably a number of identity cards, an empty wallet and a video copy of the film McNAMARA in case he forgets who he is and what he did.

Bob's intention is to enjoy the evening. Possibly only he really understands the particular variety of people that have been gathered together here. Yet his pleasure is affected by a love of strategy. While remaining thoughtful, he is precise and incisive to such an extent that it becomes difficult for him to truly relax. A balanced, relativist position allows McNamara to justify any situation. Yet he appears to make good points during discussions. These comments are marked down. A compulsive note and memo taker. Doodles on the tablecloth back up this activity. In the end he is the most compromised individual at this parallel excursion. Remaining pragmatic but guilty as hell.

Murry Wilson is the odd one out. In his plaid trousers, sports shirt and straw trilby he looks every inch the American small town man. A white vest shows up through his shirt. And if only we could see through his trousers it would be clear that his underwear is white and large enough for the fattest man but he's not particularly overweight. He carries a musical manuscript book rather than the standard tourist guide that his appearance might indicate. Pens and a metronome reveal that he is ready to write some music. A length of 2"x 1" wood is at the ready, to be used when things start to get confusing. House keys, contracts (hand-written), a diary, dictionary and some heart pills. Sitting in a house with all these other people ensures that Murry remains bemused. This frustration causes grumpiness. Yet there are other times when things start to pick up and he appears eager. All of this is cut short by his essential conservatism. When confronted with a complex proposition he can become dismissive and reticent. Horny, sweaty and stupid.

Elsie McLuhan, on the other hand, exhibits a peculiar form of dignity. This is backed up by her possession of a razor strop. She will use it if she has to. And always with back up from the Bible. She always got shirty when Marshall forgot important words from the dictionary. She wants something more than just a quiet life in the middle of nowhere. Short stories are her favourite, especially ones with a moral tone. Elsie always carries a small mirror to check on her heavy, brown, tweed clothing. And of course a matching small brown hat with a feather is perched upon her head. While she is clearly a dignified presence, there are times when she becomes argumentative to the point of pedantry. A profound woman, almost religious in the fervour of her arguments, capable of strong rhetoric yet dismissive when her determined comments are ignored or glossed over. There are some people who have even accused her of being pompous.

"A dinner is about to take place. Tomorrow everything will be different. We are flashing between the early 1800s and 1997. For those stuck in the earlier period, the mob will become the workers. In 1997 the workers revert to their old identity. A group of people has been invited for something to eat. It is probably appropriate to explain a little bit about their activities. Robert McNamara was Secretary of Defense under Kennedy and later a World Bank representative. Masaru Ibuka co-founded Sony. Elsie McLuhan, mother of Marshall McLuhan, was a public speaker specialising in moral tales. Murry Wilson was the father of Brian Wilson. Like his son, he was a songwriter, but his ambitions were thwarted. Later he attempted to live out his desires through his son's band The Beach Boys. So it seems as if we are in the company of a specific collection of people. Maybe they would be seen as secondary characters by some people, but in this context their grouping at a dinner explains why there was no change at a specific period in British history. Not just any change, but a radical, revolutionary shift. There will also be a guide to London. A guide for freethinkers. An attempt to regain control over a set of ideas that have been appropriated by people with no interest in altering the way things are. All of this takes place within the framing device of a set of parallel histories."

So to the main subject of this book and the individual whose name forms part of the title. Erasmus is late, and he is the host. Charles Darwin's older brother enjoyed a life of literary leisure. A Georgian freethinking opium eater. We follow him as he wanders around central London. Despite the fact that he does not intend to let down his dinner guests, Erasmus gets distracted. For as he walks, he comes across different sites for the development of freethinking. At these moments he stops to contemplate the contradictions inherent in his desire for libertarian development. A set of problems that are amplified by the fact that the London he finds himself in is clearly a place familiar to us as the twentieth century draws to a close. It is no longer the London of opium eaters.

Although Erasmus has avoided his own dinner engagement, he maintains communication with his guests through this book. His new-found environment is too engaging to leave. This is not as much of a problem as it might at first appear. During bouts of opium-induced insomnia Erasmus finds that he can talk to the dinner guests and they answer him back. Yet if only he had arrived in time to meet them, everything could have been different. The London explored through this book might have remained the same, it is more likely that it would have been corrupted or even improved.

So on one level this is a guide to contemporary London through the eyes of a Georgian. Yet it is also an examination of pre-Marxist positions. An ill-researched investigation of a utopian optimism that is struggling to predict the future. An attempt to cut across the nostalgia for a period that cannot really provide a model for our own. The erosion of society as we never knew it, begins and ends here. Creating both the circumstances that lead to socialism and the roots of the present re-assessment of our sense of society.

Before we begin it is important to introduce Harriet Martineau. Older than Erasmus and not weighed down with the same sense of moral order. Her influence on his ideas should not be under-estimated.

PART 4
SCENARIO
ACT 1

The stage set at this point should be quite specific. There
are a number of key aspects that are necessary to create
the right effect for the opening scene of a musical about
freethinking, discussion and time slips. The music need not
be precise. A strong Carl Stalling influence should be
emphasised. Warner Brother. The initial set will slowly
change as the characters move around, and at certain
points we should be able to see all the separate elements
simultaneously. Remember, this is a musical. It should be
bright, entertaining and memorable.

We are probably in London. Certainly close to the centre of
a large city. We should be able to see the façade of a large
house. And in front of this house there is a road. It is a wide
street, dirty, uneven and grand. Even though you can see
the exterior of the house it should also be possible to see a
table in a dining room. So it is important that the set is
organised in order for a viewer of this musical to take in the
front of a house, the interior of a house and a road, all at the
same time. A number of people will visit this house and they
are going to have dinner together.

The musical should start with some kind of song that
introduces each character. They are referred to by name, but
at this stage we have not seen what the characters look like.
This song would be sung by a chorus, or other group of
singers who are not visible on the stage. It will become clear
that a group of people have been invited for a dinner, and in
fact this introductory song is a kind of invitation in itself.

As the opening song reaches its climax you see the dinner
guests arriving at the house one by one. Each of them uses
a different mode of transport. Some arrive in horse-drawn
taxis, some in cars, others on foot. Harriet Martineau is the
first to arrive. Tall, slow, but powerful and dignified. The
lights go off for an instant. When they come on again, there
she is, standing on the front steps of the house. Robert

McNamara, former Secretary of Defense and World Bank representative, arrives in a large black car. Masaru Ibuka follows closely behind, the co-founder of Sony approaches on foot. Elsie McLuhan, mother of Marshall McLuhan comes next, arriving in a horse-drawn taxi. Murry Wilson is probably the last to appear on stage, he comes on running from the right-hand side. Briefly he appears lost, heads in the wrong direction, and then finally makes it up the stone steps and through the front door of the house. Murry is the father of Brian Wilson of the Beach Boys. In ways that are hard to define, he seems to be responsible for most of the songs and music in this show. At certain points instruments suddenly appear on the stage and he uses them while other people are singing. This takes place even though it is rarely possible to hear what Murry is playing. It is almost as if he symbolises the musical element of our story. He is so plainly dominated by the other guests in intellectual terms, that it is only through music that Murry can demonstrate a certain degree of mental and physical dexterity. Occasionally, in mid-conversation, he shows off the extent of his musical versatility. Murry always plays slightly clichéd show music, but it is relatively impressive all the same. Plodding, unimaginative but deft. A marked contrast to the strong Carl Stalling influence that otherwise dominates the score. You can never hear an entire song or complete passage when Murry plays, but the snatches of music that are audible leave a strong impression on the rest of the dinner guests. Their positive reactions, toe-tapping, smiling and nodding seem to make him idiotically happy and depressed all at the same time.

Of course the key character in this musical is Erasmus Darwin even though the title is a nod to Masaru. Erasmus is always on the move, but he remains outside the house. He never makes it inside and spends the entire musical wandering around the stage. It is important that this stage area can accommodate the illusion of many different places and moods, all culled from the centre of London and conjured up from the middle of an opium-addled brain. This means that the lighting has to be very specific, especially in the opening scene. Strong shafts of super-bright light should swing between the back and front of the set.

Flashing between the people who have arrived for the dinner and the host. Erasmus may be invisible and absent to the guests, but he is ever-present for the audience of this musical, lost and wandering round the city/stage. After all, tonight is the night that the mob become the workers, tomorrow everything will be different. It is the last chance for a complex group of people to come together across time and produce the potential for revolution. From tomorrow, Marxism is an inevitability and the power will move away from freethinking diners and into the rightful hands of working people. That's what it says in the book any way. Remember we are stuck in a time slip between Georgian London and the near future.

Erasmus is late and 100 flowers are laid out on the stage. Erasmus, in his central role, sings a little song about the time of the 100 Flowers. A moment of destructive and devastating reassessment in China during the 1950s under Mao Tse-tung. As Erasmus sings his informative song he considers each bloom. After only a few lines of the song he begins to move around the set. Erasmus considers each flower with the eyes of a curious, detached, opiated Georgian. After quite some time he takes each bloom and moves it carefully to another place on the stage. Sometimes this activity is carried out carefully, at other times he is quite rough and handles great bundles, moving them from place to place with little care and in some distress.

One of the key issues that is explored in the book ERASMUS IS LATE is the idea of a time slip. And the key reflection taking place refers to the way in which this concept is so prevalent in certain forms of entertainment media. Due to the fact that this musical is based on the book it also deals with time slips. This causes problems, but also allows certain games to be played, so throughout the destabilisation at the heart of this work, we must be able to see the house that forms the base for tonight's meal, even when action is centred elsewhere. The building is rather specific in the sense that it fits with architectural traits familiar from the Georgian period in Britain. As such, the time slip is not over-stated. The centre of London is still full of such buildings.

And apparently they were sometimes painted bright colours. So the lighting must always be considered carefully in order to make sure that the exterior of the house changes appearance throughout this musical experience. It is not necessary to describe the look of the place too carefully. It's the kind of house that has a basement which can be reached from the street. Iron railings surround the periphery of the site but because this may be impractical whenstaging an exhibition/musical, railings can also be used as a recurring decorative motif. There are some steps at the front of the house that lead up to a black door. Somehow all these things must be visible at all times, even when we are only considering the interior of the place. The windows are rather mean looking. You cannot see the frames too easily, but the back and side walls of the set are punctuated by rows of these windows, visible at certain points and invisible at other times. It should be possible to see both the interior and the exterior of this place. Therefore it is maybe necessary to construct the façade of this house from some kind of transparent material that may occasionally appear opaque and at other times transparent, depending on how the lighting is arranged and manipulated.

After the flower interlude we are left with Erasmus standing near to the front of the stage locked in one position, telling his story and introducing all the people who have arrived at his house. Acting like a narrator. Clearly he is not going to arrive at the same time as the guests but it is not certain at this point that he will never make it to this important dinner date. Only people who have read the book ERASMUS IS LATE will truly understand the circumstances that surround the absence of the central character. It is sufficient to say that at this moment in the musical we cannot be sure whether he will join his guests or not. This is the key element of dramatic irony that sustains the traditional element of this narrative construction. The guests are arriving and you see them go into the house and take their places around a large table. Everyone introduces themselves to each other. We cannot hear exactly what they are saying but each dinner guest appears to behave in a specific accepted and familiar way. They are all polite to each other and seem reasonably happy to meet. There is, however, a certain degree of visible tension. This tension is manifest in different, quite subtle forms. For example through the way in which people nervously wipe their hands before meeting or look each other up and down (when they have the opportunity to do this without appearing to be rude). It is clear from this complex body language that they are all wondering where their host could have got to. And it is clear to all of us that he is lost in the middle of the set moving flowers around and thinking about various mid-twentieth-century collapses. All linked to degraded utopias. Erasmus moves around but cannot really make contact with any of these people. He is speaking to himself at all times, but somehow he is also communicating with the others. While he is talking, music starts to play and all the people in the dining room acknowledge each other's presence in a resigned and relatively open way. The introductions are over. As the guests settle down to their evening of discussion and dinner, Erasmus wanders about at the front of the stage area.

This is when the second key character introduces herself. Harriet Martineau. At first it seems as if she will begin with a song, but after a couple of bars of music and a big build up she forces the music to stop (by waving her hands and shaking her head) and instead speaks directly and informatively, past the dinner guests and out towards an audience. Erasmus interrupts and, although Harriet continues to talk, calmly and clearly, his voice drowns hers out. The reason for this is that Erasmus wants and needs to present her to everyone. Her unheard monologue and his introduction end simultaneously. As Erasmus bows away towards the back of the set Harriet finally lets the music begin by gesturing with her hands and sings a little song about the fact that she's feeling depressed and that she's been doing too much work and that she might try a move to the countryside. Although she normally likes going to these kinds of gatherings, tonight Harriet is sure that this is not going to be an enjoyable evening. This could be a source of some tension between Erasmus and her, but he is too out of it to notice or really respond effectively to her potential dissatisfaction. For Harriet, salmon suppers and debate with

Erasmus have been central to the development of her essays, pamphlets, complex rhetoric and paradoxically hard-line Libertarianism. She is reaching the point where there is a recognition of a set of contradictions that she can no longer tolerate or juggle with. The main visible result of this unease is that Harriet tends to speak as if she is the only person in the room. She does not engage in real dialogue. She is rather upset that Erasmus is not at home, but the source of her real fury is the fact that she senses that tomorrow the mob will become the workers and this is something that fills her with fear. For while she believes people tend towards upward mobility, it is non-hierarchical organisation that she rejects most firmly.

The reactions of the other guests at this point are rather weak. They don't immediately warm to Harriet due to her 'special relationship' with Erasmus and the rather cavalier way in which she is ignoring them in favour of the attempt to make direct contact with the absent opium-addled host. This set of problems are compounded when Harriet starts to talk about her Libertarian beliefs, her complete lack of faith in state control and her fear of the rise of the workers, which she cannot truly understand because it is yet to take place, but she senses will undermine her position. Harriet talks about multiple positions as a way of combating this effect. In addition she desperately tries to address the idea that nothing is certain or fixed, but from her Georgian, early-nineteenth-century position it is hard for her to use such flexibility. The other guests smile politely and some even begin to acknowledge the sad complexity that lies at the root of what she is saying.

Erasmus is starting to move around the stage. A shopfront is suddenly illuminated and the rest of the lights fade down a little. We realise that Erasmus is considering a particular shop from the late-twentieth century. An electronics shop. The kind of place that stocks every type of computer, camera and brand of discounted hi-fi equipment. And for the first time he begins to sing. His voice is a bit of a shock. A high-pitched falsetto. He rapidly outlines a story of overlapping ideas and communication while he sings about the future. At certain points he takes an opium pastille. This slows him down a little, and lowers the pitch of his voice, but within a couple of lines he is soaring once again. When singing he lacks any obvious signs of emotion, his voice belies his rather wrecked exterior. Erasmus sings about moving around through time and the fact that he can't deal with relative positions. He cannot cope with modern ideas about having multiple positions and a rather complicated, layered view of things. Yet he can understand why these multiple positions might develop, in fact he is the conduit between the two eras under consideration in this musical. It is Erasmus who stands at the centre. He is symbolic of a period that created the conditions that allowed for both Marxism and free-market positions. Standing caught between these two areas pleases him greatly. As his song ends the first act of our musical draws to a close with a monologue from Erasmus directed at the audience.

The lights start to come up in the dining room of the house. And everyone is having an animated conversation. They remain oblivious to the presence of their high pitched host.

Erasmus addresses everyone:
"But as we have discovered, days are not the same and if they are not even tied together by some thread of continuity, is nothing located? At least general trends might be predictable. That's the way it has been until now. Yet I fear that these undercurrents that permit a degree of rationalisation are merely coincidence. And on the trail of some opium I think even less in those fixed slightly progressive terms. I am permitted to time slip into your mode of multiple referencing. But it is not your theoretical freewheeling, my version of multi-vision merely apes a-historicism. No cultural kleptomania. My time slip is based on what could be and not on some existential set of total referencing that may lead to inactivity." (From ERASMUS IS LATE.) And as he finishes this speech the lights come up really brightly, and you see all the people, including Erasmus, locked on stage. They are no longer moving but fixed in anticipation of what will take place. A loud crescendo of music indicates the end. Fade the lights to black.

ACT 2

The second act opens with deafening traffic noise which gradually starts to calm down. Specific lighting effects allow for silhouettes of cars and trucks to be projected across the set. The glow of a shop window is quite a clear focus point. You can also see the dinner guests, whose set has now been dragged towards the back of the performance area. They are only lightly illuminated, as if by candlelight. The façades of four more shops, all slightly similar to the first, gradually fade up from the darkness of the set. It soon becomes apparent that Erasmus is with us again, lurking around the shop windows. He is obviously in no hurry and takes his time as he studies the different signs that decorate the shopfronts. These logos in the form of names are also projected around the set. Each one alludes to a specific electronics company. Erasmus seems fascinated by all these clear and powerful signs. As he walks around he begins to hear music. A chorus of people, none of whom are visible on the stage, hum a song that involves the names and objects that he can see in the five sites for the developments of electronic communication that are now available to him.

The lights fade down and attention turns back to the guests. Murry leaves the table and takes us on a walk down a narrow passageway. A staircase is visible on one side. He looks around as he walks, and checks the varied architectural features of the house. It is not a type of building that he is familiar with, he seems a little confused, while also appreciating the place. All this time we can hear loud sounds of conversation coming from the dining room. Murry's exploratory interlude is accompanied by music.

As Murry walks, the dining room element of the set moves towards the front of the stage. The table is now clearly visible. It is heavy and made of wood, covered with a clean white cloth and fairly empty considering the importance of tonight's dinner. There is a mantelpiece with photographs, drawings and some pottery. Murry is still temporarily distracted by his exploratory mood. He is somehow guiding us through the house, while Erasmus starts to sing a song, also guiding in his own opium-addled way. The words are a reminder that it is important to think about the way in which society is constructed. And that he will try and lead us into territories that are very vivid. Too difficult to deal with. All this will happen without straying too far from his home. So it becomes clear from this song why everything must remain visible simultaneously within this set. Erasmus sings about how he is not interested in man developing fitness for anything. So he is not concerned with the classic interpretation of evolution because he believes that man has already transcended such a state and entered a period where there is a degree of free will involved in decision making that ensures a particular unevenness. Also Erasmus has a major problem dealing with any of these things, because the theory of evolution has not yet been developed. So (by default Philippe) he is more interested in un-fitness and under-achievement. He is singing about how exciting it would be if you could enter a state of continual reconsideration rather than a simple, straightforward way of looking at the world. He cannot think in relativistic terms or flash around through time as well as others but he will be able to later. Erasmus admits that in order to do this he will need some new starting points. And maybe it is becoming clear that this guide, walking around shops and other places, also this non-appearance at the dinner, have got something to do with creating a new way of looking at the world. Or at the very least a new way of creating some starting points in order to help us devise a way to live, an alternative to the rise of free-market thinking. It's the last chance for a revolution. Erasmus admits that he is engaged in a faded analysis, or rather a blurry analysis. He is standing caught between shopfronts, moving this way and that. He can't decide which way to go.

Without warning Erasmus turns towards the dinner guests, the lights come on in the dining room and all the guests turn towards him. It is clear from the way they move their heads and scan the set that they cannot actually see him. But somehow they can hear him. Erasmus once more and the music drops to a very sinister and low tempo. Erasmus begins to sing. The words to the song are complicated. And there is no mistaking the seriousness of his message.

One option here
is for us to chase
a consistent level of ongoing invention.
This is supposed to occur
and, while change has been slow,
it has not been imperceptible.

Certainly when keeping in mind
what goes on beyond the kind of discussion
that tends to take place at a dinner like this.
Maybe, concerning what was said earlier,
we are in fact taking part in the construction
of a whole new series of tiny moral frameworks
that guide our actions
instead of some grand, overwhelming and therefore
rather clumsy idea.

This proposal would seem reasonable,
seeing as it is always being adapted
by the most dynamic people,
although to link ourselves
with such groups
may be dangerous at this stage.

Erasmus repeats the last lines a couple of times. There is a sense in which the conclusion of Act 2 is rather different to the first. There is no clear climax or musical crescendo. The secondary lights and the plaintive singing just fade away. We are left with Erasmus standing in the middle of the road. The final spots fade down. And you can see that all the guests are rather concerned as the dining room is swallowed up by the encroaching darkness, they know something has been said but they are not exactly clear who said it. The 'unheard' song had a profound effect, but it was communicated without clarity, direction or true comprehension. Murry, Masaru, Robert, Elsie and Harriet are disturbed and unsettled by the developments tonight.

ACT 3

This time only one of the shopfronts is visible and we are also confronted by a big traffic island in the middle of the set, positioned right at the very front. And Erasmus is standing there on the traffic island, clearly visible to any kind of audience. You cannot see the dinner guests any more. Due to lighting and the use of some screens which have been pulled in front of the dining room area. Some kind of projection has been made onto the back wall. This gives us a detailed view of Erasmus. His hair is long and grey, combed back off his forehead and seems to extend seemlessly into bushy grey sideburns. He has taken off his tophat and holds it in his hands. The music at this stage has become really quite loud. There is no singing, just Erasmus, stuck, locked onto this traffic island. All the focus should really be on him at this point. We are entering a period of reminiscence. He starts to recall his background and especially his childhood. The large projection on the back wall starts to shift and we are allowed to see what he is thinking. This process is quite straightforward. When he thinks about his brother you see an image of his brother. A transparently dumb way of presenting a set of memories but quite in keeping with the opium-laced absent central character. Many other images are projected. A house in the country and a house in the city are obviously important for him. A university in Edinburgh and a college in the centre of London. A house, a tunnel system. The Poster Studio and Richard Wolff's film studio. All these images indicate a past in a rather hollow, sloppy way. During this period, Erasmus does not talk and he does not sing. But you can see varied images and hear loud music. The sounds are extremely variable, including a soundtrack for the 'Snow Dancing' party.

Towards the end of this sequence, you realise that some people are moving around behind him. They are wearing 'snaking suits', a bit like wetsuits that have been altered. Long tails have been added to these outfits. The people who are wearing them crawl along the floor, using their arms in order to move, swinging their tails from side to side. This is the best way for them to travel across the set. They are never clearly visible, but remain in the middle distance. Erasmus is blind to this activity but it does seem to make him a little more agitated. It is as if they were a rather clumsy illustration of an Erasmus idea. It is about time that he snapped out of his reverie and thankfully he begins to talk about the shop windows. This is clearly one of the key elements of his absence that really interests him. He describes the displays and tries to explain the fact that he doesn't completely understand what they are and what they are for. He talks about the idea of debate. And reveals that he is not so sure what is going to happen tonight in the house or on his tour. He is particularly drawn to the shopfront that carries the sign 'Microworld', Erasmus finds the name funny. After enough opium, anyone could get sucked into this discussion of shops and electronic communication.

Very slowly the screens hiding the diners have been pulled back and the lights are fading up. You can now see all the dinner guests once more. The traffic island starts to slide towards the back of the stage area and while this is happening the house stays where it is, but the dining room area separates away and slides towards the front of the set. This allows us to study all of the parallel people. The others. As the dining room locks to the front of the stage the table starts to rotate and each person gets up in turn and comes to stand where Erasmus had been on the traffic island. With a full spotlight you have a chance to study each of them. The American man with the glasses and the bald head. The Japanese technologist and prototype fetishist. The American musician and frustrated songwriter. 'Two Step Side Step'. The Canadian public speaker and finally Harriet, with her stiff, English attitude that fits so well with a desire for radical Libertarian development. A development that none of them truly want. If they did, they would do something tonight. But they fear the worst. Not the people who will come later, but the true Georgians. For Erasmus and Harriet will leave the right conditions for the development of contradictory socio-political impulses.

After the inspection process, the guests return to their places at the dinner table. Murry comes forward and explains that he is really happy to be at the dinner, after a short time he begins to hum a stupid, happy but not unpleasant tune. Then he begins to sing about how pleased he is with the way in which the evening is going and what a privilege it is for him to be included at a salmon supper like this. Fortunately the focus begins to shift once more to Erasmus who throughout this time has been wandering around in a rather nervous and increasingly clumsy way. He is heading for a collapse. Full of opium and frightened to face up to what is going to take place. Erasmus can remember the future. Always moving towards the back of the stage. A spotlight follows him as he wanders around and Murry continues to hum his stupid song. Erasmus is moving and Murry turns his attention to the mantelpiece. Inspecting each item in turn. The other guests are smiling at him, they find his actions amusing. So will the father of Brian Wilson really inherit all this potential and pass it on to his son? I get around is, after all, Erasmus's current motto.

Erasmus is agitated, staggering around in near darkness. Still moving between one shop and another towards the back of the stage. He flickers between exhaustion and elation. The lighting at this point is completely out of control. Suddenly, without warning, McNamara stands up and everyone stops what they were doing. McNamara makes a very powerful speech, powerful because it sounds so reasonable. He talks about the idea of the individual. And the way the individual has been rationalised in western cultures. He also talks about the fact that whenever you try and analyse something in a new way you tend to lay down certain fixed points because there is no other way you can proceed. And although the specific things you talk about in your analysis may not be so interesting for people, those little markers and spots that you leave behind, those moments of minor conclusion are really useful for the development of further debate. These micro-conclusions are the powerful elements of analysis and they can really alter the way in which people consider society. It is possible that he is claiming to be more interested in structure than content. This is because he is rather worried about using metaphors and cannot cope with symbolic rationalisations. This is clearly not such a problem for the other people, but it really worries McNamara. He starts reflecting upon Erasmus's actions tonight. Somehow he is now functioning as a commentator. Taking stock of the whole situation. Talking the ideas of a parallel historian. Someone from the past who operates as 'The Other Man', someone who works alongside other people but is not quite at the centre of things. With certain situations, people can get stuck, feeling that things happen to them and not the other way round. McNamara explains how he feels very close to this mode of behaviour. He can really appreciate what Erasmus is doing. But the more he tries to plead sympathy with Erasmus, talking about Malthus and other Georgian thinkers, the more animated and agitated Erasmus becomes. As things really get going, he starts marching around towards the back of the stage and just occasionally coming forwards. When Erasmus moves to the front he stares hard at McNamara before going back and resuming his avoidance.

The others take their turns on the traffic island. Every time someone comes forward to speak about their ideas, as McNamara is doing at the moment, Erasmus comes up really close to them and checks them out extremely carefully. This activity seems to give him pleasure. It is as if they were all trying to work something out, to understand, but they cannot see their host. Maybe he holds the key to future events. There will be no revolution. Erasmus is happy just to look at the people he brought together for this one night. At this point, for example, he is going through McNamara's pockets. While unable to completely control his guests, he can at least examine and absorb them. This process begins to overwhelm him. He starts to try and interrupt and he wins the 'talk the loudest competition for volume with his piercing falsetto. This is inevitable even though the other others cannot hear him. Erasmus, as always, drowning everyone out with talk of opium and freethinking.

PART 5

CONCLUSION
GO HOME

… Dumping goods on other markets. A technique employed to ensure the corruption of that longed-for fantasy of free trade and exchange. It has been a recurring sub-text. A matter of great concern to all the people here. Well, maybe not for Murry, but even he is starting to believe that he is part of this free-market dynamic. After all, it is people like him who will defend it most rigorously, even while hiding behind a protectionist position that would stun Erasmus, if he were to truly understand it.

The white table cloth is stained. Some of the guests have even made notes directly onto its surface. It seems as if this house has no note paper. There is a rumour that later in life, or was it earlier, Erasmus wrote some poetry. This may be true, but he certainly wasn't writing much at the time of this meal. Near the beginning of the supper there had been a search for paper and pens at a point when Masaru felt it necessary to explain the u-shaped pricing curve. Despite Elise's thorough search through the house not a single scrap of paper or any writing implements could be found. Fortunately Bob had a pen, so they began to work straight onto the table cloth. Elsie didn't approve, Harriet loved the idea, McNamara thought it a practical solution, Masaru was no longer paying attention and Murry didn't care either way.

And we can see them all sitting there. The question of whether or not they have eaten anything is irrelevant to the narrative. Erasmus is still trying to communicate.

"Yes, yes." Erasmus is warming up, and so late in the day. "Guilds, apprentices and societies. But not the workers. An optimism prevailed and it is one that still exists for me. A belief in development—that people stuck in a specific social crisis will rise above it. A relative growth, based on freethinking and lack of overwhelming control. I enjoy hearing your people harking back to a time before their confused attempts at social responsibility. We believed that people would help themselves but we could not imagine how they would do it. The ideas shifted across the Atlantic and the Channel. We could not imagine them using our terminology. The development of a language that can deal with the concept of communication. Something to be subjected to and something to involve yourself in. The adjustment of Elysian utopias into materialist utopias. The variability and mutability of non-conformist theory. A degree of pragmatism. And we had it all. Ecology. Biology. Technology and a lump of opium dissolved. Toying with another salmon supper." ... (cont.)

So there was a book concerning a dinner and now there could be a musical too. Part of a structure that has been rearranged and is now open to further adaptation using this new book as a guide. Looking for parallel positions and playing within the spaces that are opened up as a result of this approach. IBUKA! is rather closely connected to an attempt to come to terms with an entertainment media that frequently focus upon time slips as an essential part of its construction but also it is just a potential musical/exhibition. IBUKA! could be done. Yet it is not necessary to research every part. A reading of the book ERASMUS IS LATE could already set up a number of possibilities. IBUKA! Come into the office with a pair of headphones taped to your head and everything will become clear.

THE WINTER SCHOOL
Produced as a print in the form of a magazine layout this short text was produced to coincide with Documenta X in 1997. It describes a fictional moment in 1971 when it might have been possible to redirect Documenta towards a permanent 'school' or event that would replace the existing five-year cycle of exhibitions. The work was secreted in the Documenta archive for 1971 and made available as this print. Some of the ideas within it came into fruition with the unitednationsplaza project for a free school in Berlin in 2006.

THE WINTER SCHOOL

Last year. 1996. A winter scenario. Before the main event. A moment spared for thinking back to another time. 1971. A new structure could have been created, a kind of school. A place to set action into action. A projection into the near future. Changing everything. It's just that no one can remember the details. Three people are looking for the original report. And they'll have to shift and flicker in order to reclaim that old forward thinking.

It's 1971. In a room, overlooking the lake, a series of reports are being written. But we only have access to fragments of this emerging structure. The voice of the report coordinator is indistinct and presently hard to identify. For the moment we will only be able to make out the first few lines. First a cough and then: "Discussion Island is a lost Celtic place, no longer missing. Clans maintained this shared site, each taking turns to farm it in yearly rotation. In the event of any dispute between them, people gathered on Discussion Island to thrash out and reorganise crisis. An example of a desire for negotiated solutions that is part of a suppressed history. In parallel to this we now have a report that exposes an interest in people and situations where the location for action and analysis is focused upon the centre. A reclamation of the near future through an understanding of the middle ground."

It's 1996. If you want to find the centre of things then go to sleep. Not a coma sleep, but an active break towards reorganisation. In this story there are three people, all heading off in different directions. We will see their travels and feel the complexity of their negotiations. They are trying to think ahead. They are all trying to reclaim the idea of projection. Projection as a tool, the predictive meanderings that maintain us all within a state of thrall. Reclaiming the near future at a time when we might believe that there is no point. And the first person is dreaming, if that is what it should be called. Half asleep and half awake. We are dealing with an individual this time. There are no longer any groups. Half asleep and half awake. Slipping thoughts. There is no bed here but everything is comfortable enough. We are a long way from any cities. A great distance from any other buildings. But there is no isolation this time. There are only fragments in the sleep state. And it is a half-sleep and half-wake that is only sustained by small possibilities and elements of negotiation. So the first person is only half with us. Thinking about a number of objects and images from the recent past. In order to move ahead, it might be necessary to reflect just before the slumber. A good time for addressing those things that have only just happened. It seems as if this is the first person's role. It is a good moment to start a winter school. Off season, out of sync.

It's still 1971. And on the lake outside the report room a man is struggling with a boat. It's distracting. Turning from the window and away from those concerns, a little more of the report may now be read. "So we are exposed to a persistent use of the phrase 'the middle ground'. It is important to understand such a term in relation to the socio-economic structure of the society in general and necessary to trap it in a report that is caught within a fiction. The middle ground, a broad, expanding area where you find negotiation, strategy, bureaucracy, compromise, planning and projection. An area long recognised as that which is crucial to maintaining the deferment of solutions that lies at the heart of the liberal capitalist dynamic of promise and potential."

It's 1996. Something must be started. Images and objects from the recent past. Pens, televisions and trousers? A series of questions leads to the problem of whether or not there is the real possibility of seeing any of these things clearly any longer. At least that's the problem for this first person. So let's slip away from the difficulties and the person that bears them and move around the outside of the place where the first person is caught between at least two states. We are circling the area of awaking. Now it is more like thinking aloud, but without the moving or speaking. Clear and precise. If only someone would arrive and explain that there is very little time left. There has to be a winter school. That is clear at least. An antidote within a series of shared moments, a smile plays across the person's lips as their thoughts turn to incomplete stratagems, all of them developing around a beautiful, decorated fir tree.

We approach that first person again. But this time, we start from quite a distance and we move in fast. Picking up the pace. It's as if we hadn't noticed before, there is a panel overhead. Multiple and bright colours are working away. Caught in the middle ground. Half awake. Half not awake. While considering the implications of bureaucracy, compromise and negotiation. As we know by now, the first person is trying to be more precise and those thoughts are slipping once again. Try and pin down some moments where a winter school can work. Just before the main events. 1971, a year to remember. Now try that list again. A Brionvega television, a Bic biro, velvet or corduroy? Try to collate a complete list of the things you would need in order to break through a progression of ideas. Times when the winter school could have gone into action but no one had a timetable. Leave the first person for a while. Under a canopy, safe and sound, everything is happening.

It's 1971. Away from the window a fire is now roaring. And the report coordinator places something vague into the flames. Holding a fixed gaze while the yellow flicker licks at an ambiguity. Just to see what will happen. A little test. A little boredom? Heat builds up and then a shout from the lake pulls the reporter back to attention. Read on. "This area is enormous and attempts to embrace us all. It is presented as the way things are but is clearly fought for. Put forward as the equilibrium into which structures naturally fall but clearly needs maintenance and continual action to keep it broad. The central zone is well recognised and in its earlier form was fought through the establishment of clear-cut battle lines with which to attack the bourgeois sensibilities that were seen to prop it up. We all know this form of barricade development. And we also know it is useless as a straight forward tool."

It's 1996 again. So shift away from number one and embrace mobility. Move through a series of streets. There are elements of the situation and environment that are recognisable. All of these elements need to be described. But some of the objects that we come across appear to function in parallel to our sense of the present. Yet, there has to be some attempt to list it all down. A catching of all the parts and pieces. This task will have to be done before the winter school can really get under way.

The second person is in a bar. Pan around it for a minute or two. Dark crescents under every eye. They look up and away. This person came in about three minutes ago and made a winding, interrupted trip to the bar. Stopping frequently to look and greet people. The second person is speaking to everyone they come across today. Talking up to the limit of distance and prepared to press on. And at every point there is some drawing back. A neat technique to defer the speaking process. All promise. They don't realise that the bar is not public, it's private. On the way through and out the other side, it soon becomes clear that the bar is part of a house. Away on the other side is a work place, somewhere for the second person to get things done. Someone who thinks ahead at all times. For it is the moment to come up with a number of future scenarios. But hide them. Conceal them for a while, behind the familiarity of such engaging company.

We're back in 1971. Something has to happen in the winter time. Is there more in the fragmented report? "This broad swathe of activity is generally seen as anything other than valuable territory for investigation. It is not mimicking the engagements of the middle ground that I am interested in, but the possibility of investigating the thrall within which the middle ground of strategised projection holds the potentially dynamised social and political structures that surround us. And along with any understanding of the middle ground must come a time-based conception of the role social and economic projection has played in guiding the development of our situation. A day to day addiction to trends and the forecasting."

It's 1996 for the last time and soon to be 1997. The third person is in an aeroplane travelling across a developed, well-marked landscape. This person is making a series of mental sidesteps all of which look towards alternative options in relation to the landscape below. This person also investigates the possibility of expansion rather than merely development. All of these ideas are noted on a number of sick bags with a borrowed pen. Things are moving faster now. We cut between the first, second and third person increasingly quickly. They start to argue and contradict each other without ever meeting. They are faced with no option and they are coming together. Closer and closer. It is winter and they arrive in a city. They pass each other at the station without recognition and head off in different directions towards the flat muted tones of the immediate countryside. The Winter School is no longer only an option, it is a necessity.

1971. And in the house by the lake the sky is darkening. The days are short at this time of year. The report will be finished soon. Out of sync. But just in time.

DISCUSSION ISLAND/
BIG CONFERENCE CENTRE
Turning away from the idea of specific historical characters
towards processes, DISCUSSION ISLAND is a story that
sweeps across various locations and situations in order to
create a complex picture of how decisions are made at a
point where there is no strong shared ideological concensus
about how the future should be. Or, to put it another way,
how decisions are made during a period when people
have been told that no collective progressive set of ideas
are possible ,nor can such ideas ever find a stable form.
Looking at structural questions and detailed moments,
DISCUSSION ISLAND starts in the new big conference centre
of the title. A large space within the building has gone
unplanned and unnoticed in the new building in order to
create a crisis, which will permit some degree of freedom
within the planned structure. With this book the artworks
related to it occurred both before and after the writing of the
text and in many cases set the scene for a text that had few
clear locations.

DISCUSSION ISLAND/
BIG CONFERENCE CENTRE

CONCILIATION

However hard you try it's always tomorrow. And now it's here again. Across the other side of town trauma had overwhelmed personal exchange. Something self-willed and determined had cut through the dusk. Pain in a building. We all called it The Big Conference Centre. It probably had another name in honour of somebody seriously compromised, but to us it was just The Big Conference Centre. And up on top there was a room. Twenty-second floor. Big, airy and false-ceilinged. Windows down to the floor. Clad in silencing carpet. Up there, the day before yesterday, someone had finally done it. Lost in the place, caught and alone, they had repeatedly run full pelt against the reinforced glass of that best top room. Minor personal damage like bruising and broken teeth must have gone unnoticed in the repetitive drive for fresh air and dramatic absence. As far as anyone can make out he needed at least ten attempts. Moving faster and faster with each flailing run-up. Breathing hard and determined. And then on the eleventh impact, the glass gave way. Crashing open and falling away to allow brutal passage and moments of weightlessness on the way to physical chaos below. Numbed initially from the repeated window impact, our crasher came to a new form of consciousness half-waydown. The pavement concrete stayed where it was and didn't move up to meet him and his smile. Well, they said it was like a grin, although fuck knows how anyone could be sure with a flattened face buried in the top of a Toyota like that.

Now everything is different. There is access to tomorrow. But before our corporate entry can be validated we need some background. A reminder of quieter times. Way outside the city, close to a National Park. A house without fencing to define the edges of its base. A building growing fresh from a grassy lump surrounded by conifers. Inside now, we walked into a room with Coca-Cola coloured walls. The floor had been laid down some time ago. Planks of wood nailed discreetly to a concealed series of solid chunked supports. The widest were certainly no less than that measure of a palm, the narrowest were at most only three fingers broad. The original putting down of this floor planking had been precise and complete. And now combined with walls the colour of Coca-Cola. Not the whole wall, but certainly the top three quarters of each, not including the area around the windows, or the last small strip before the ceiling is reached. Back to the wooden boards that formed the flooring. Over a period of some years, could be at least one hundred, the wood had become blackened beyond dirty. Despite renovation of the room, this beyond dirt had been allowed to build up. No real effort had been made to clean it or to balance out the surface shade. Not that it wasn't smooth, unevenness was purely down to look rather than feel. The smoothness of the worn wood was as consistent as the multi-toned colour was varied. While any remains of non-domestic debris had always been removed, no attempt was ever made to begin a form of unification through cleaning. In any case, the only option would be to sand down the entire surface and start again with glass-paper and varnish. Someone had decided that wasn't an option quite some time ago. Not a loss of choice through difficulty, but a decision based on retaining an antiqued look. The floor was a useful indicator of the authenticity of this house. Showing off elderly qualities exposed through revelation of construction. A little sign of age to be understood and appreciated. It was never intended as something to marvel at, yet it had been placed, trimmed and finished in such a way as to indicate that it might always be on view, then and now. Not that the floor should ever have been worthy of comment, praise or rejection, rather that its visibility was always going to be a marker. An indication that someone had cared deeply about this isolated building. A crafted island of hardwood in a complex zone of super nature.

All the following things happen at the same time. Lincoln is walking down the edge of an urban highway when a man hits the roof of a Toyota. And here we have the start of a time-coded section. A parallelism as three people start to work in sync with each other. It will be important to deal with each separately and in turn. Lincoln, a person who works in the middle. Moving towards an attempt to address some of the problems inherent in gathering together a picture of the projected near future through the use of tools that will come from the centre. Relational tools. A concentration upon issues that operate between the straightforward equivalence of intentions and results. There is some specificity here but only in the background. In order to negotiate the commencement of this thinking Lincoln has decided to set up a think tank. Initially the process could be straightforward. A building might be acquired, and inside there should be a special room. Somewhere nearly private. And crashing out through that window far above the rush of traffic comes somebody, soon to be somebody's body.

There's a mountain in the middle of a small country. The state autonomy here was a natural fringe benefit of geography. The mountain range that features our peak has been used as a natural border since 1123. There were always people convinced that geology was a way to solve the problem of how to divide one territory from another. The mountain is pretty steep because the rest of the land is flat. Right down to sea level in places. In fact, just out to the south-west of the mountain there are parts of this country that fall below zero. So although the mountain is only 3,000 metres high, it feels bigger. And it's rarely cold at the top. No skiing here, instead, half-way up, people build modest little houses with underground car parking. It's not a bad place to live, yet most use it as a location for second or even third homes. Our mountain was never a site of primary production, not even of sheep. If you take a train out there, the closest city to the western base is at the end of a rail line. Then you can rent a car, especially if it's a Tuesday in June, after all, it had happened before. Ramsgate has been missing for some years. A semi-comatose half-dreamer who has never met Lincoln. At some point Lincoln had visited this part of the world. And recently returned once more, but this is Ramsgate's moment and he's not really ready for contact.

A bird flies bang into an apartment window while someone inside is distracted by a smoke alarm. Another fine day in the city. Work is going on to prop up a burnt-out video store. The way this place developed ensured that conference centres were never very important. Anyway, they're usually deployed as a boost. The middle of this town was never reduced to abandonment. So the conference centre couldn't be used as a way to revitalise a place that had otherwise found itself in a dormant state. They built it anyway. But who would want organised speaking? Diverse groups travelling great distances to confirm their findings and improve their motivation. No way would an urban mess like this appeal to them. Too intuitive, too functional. So the people who conceived the conference centre knew before they had even begun that it had to be a precise structure. Covert and corporate. Let's speak to Ron for a while. He works in the urban conference centre. He can talk within a mannered code of speaking. A comforting person to act as a describer, locked into his belief in buildings. While in the background we know three protagonists are getting on with something differently important. At least their work has some significance for the state of development and development of the state, even if Ron is not yet aware of it. Ramsgate, Lincoln and Denmark are up and away. Each has some groundwork to do before we may return to their thing. And the best place for that is in the air. Each checks in, baggage logged and weighed. A walk down that thumping ramp and inside the carefully panelled aluminium. Plastic flexibility soon to be creaking against ribbed superstructure.

Ramsgate is dreaming, half asleep and half awake. Thinking about a number of objects and images from the recent past. A panel is over his head. Slipping thoughts. 1971/1985/1997. Walking now in the street there are elements of the situation and the environment that are recognisable. All are described, but some are clearly parallel rather than definable as familiar. That's his work for now. Complex description of the present and its close relations.

Lincoln is in the bar up in the first-class section. Talking with people but thinking ahead, coming up with a number of future scenarios while at the same time maintaining a series of fairly ordinary conversations. Three specific examples of taking an idea through development to a number of micro-conclusions are outlined. He just alters the order of engagement. Testing and tempting, trying out some scenarios.

Denmark is in an aeroplane travelling across a developed, well-marked landscape. Making a series of mental side steps all of which look towards alternative options in relation to the landscape below. Investigating the possibility of expansion rather than mere development. All of his ideas are noted on a number of sick bags with a borrowed pen. Turbulence. Each of them grabs the nearest reassurance. A table, a leg and a glass.

We cut between all three increasingly quickly. Each one in turn appears to reach a point where compromise is the option that offers the most mobile position, keeps a dream going, allows a conversation to continue and avoids error. The necessity to communicate is what leads to this temporary sense of negotiated give and take.

Ramsgate turns on the video screen in the seat back in front of him. Off-white plastic housed in a padded tartan cushion. Turned on, there is a chance to return to the semi dream-state. Take note of interior dialogue.

There's a doubled irony here. But then I'm asleep on an aeroplane. It is often assumed, probably quite correctly, that if a political strategist claims to believe in anything their statement should be interpreted as part of a sceptical web of ideas wrapped up in layers of dark humour. A scenario is playing itself out. It has been argued that each of us exposes most eloquently the guilty acknowledgement that all our moral and ethical structures have imploded. The way we communicate is therefore open to endless interpretation and scrutiny. Strategists can do this because the best of us operate in between other disciplines. Yet that process began at a point when the findings being proposed by the most interesting, and therefore radical, political strategists, had to be seen in the context of a general tendency towards not believing that resulted from an increasing loss of trust in control systems. This process probably came to a head in the 1960s, especially in America. Some examples are required. Lee Harvey Oswald may well have killed President Kennedy alone, but the city of Dallas provided the context within which it was possible to hate a rich Catholic Liberal chief executive and not feel abnormal. As a result, at the moment of Kennedy's assassination, his closest aides, O'Donnell and O'Brien for example, and even Clint Hill, referred to the killer in the plural, although they were pretty sure that there had only been one marksman. Remember that the city was crawling with hate. A perverse ultra-conservatism had taken hold which represented belief as a thing in itself. Order had become a fetish beyond the content of any known legal system. Law and justice had become personalised belief systems. Each individual wandering around and acting as a solo representative of justice. This attitude in the wrong place leads to murder. Many cultural phenomena from the 1960s represented a fight against that kind of thinking. Rejecting the structuring and personalisation of order for its own sake. The result was a rise in the potential of sub-cultural and pan-cultural scepticism. Flames fanned by the development of global communications and an image of the mainstream on television that could be a source for reaction as much as entertainment. Over the years since, there has been no equivalent paradigm shift in authority, yet the quality of control has changed, and we are left with only the old tools of scepticism and irony, which are no longer good enough. Freedom of expression has replaced freedom to apply justice. An exchange has been effected, and now we have a domination of scepticism attempting to shadow-box an enemy which has long since feinted out of range. The challenge for us, and challenge is always a good hammered-to-death word to use in relation to political allusions, is to find a way through the resulting equation. The interviewee smiles at the camera.

The television programme is good, but not enough to keep Ramsgate's full internal dialogue functioning. Attention lapses. A channel change is necessary, but on the other side there is only more of the same.

If you are not entirely happy with the way things are then the options are no longer clear. Ironic non-belief is an accepted stance now, so where do you look to for action? One option is to try and address the vast central area that includes bureaucracy, compromise, conciliation and so on. Not to illustrate those things, but to address them. To look carefully at the mechanics of our political and economic context without resorting to irony or distance. Not to make that vast compromised central area into a subject but to move inside the thinking and add to the confusion. The issue of believe versus don't believe is part of the binary thinking even reinforced by television programmes like MASH. It is part of the age of the enlisted person, where not believing was central to surviving within a contradictory system, that is chaos (war) produced by order (armies). It is not surprising that a lot of people have a problem with the way that they are encouraged to analyse their relative position when they are continually forced away from a clear view of the dominant centre.

The plane bumps and jogs, slipping, then regaining stability.

Whatever differences existed between your actual activities at the Pentagon and the rhetoric surrounding them seems to have melted. Of course such understanding comes as a fringe benefit of hindsight. I cannot help feeling, however, that our words fail to explain much while perfectly illustrating a sensibility that allows a precision randomness. Is this a sense of adventure or an inescapable love of obscurantics?

A double vodka. Two small plastic bottles and a glass full of ice. Up front, the pilot smiles.

Our work does not rest on empirical research or overt reliance on quasi-psychological prediction, and that's a good thing. In the last five years we have worked on three main projects. Firstly a report; secondly the establishment of two coordinated think tanks and thirdly the current project which is an attempt to address the notion of projection from the central zone of murky control, rather than the extreme fringe of possibilities. Always clear, silhouetted against the glare of the unimaginable. Unravelling the desire to maintain an illusion of improvement. Tomorrowism is a central tenet of the late-twentieth-century western capitalist dynamic. All our post-1967 research demonstrates very little interest in battling for the realm of explanation. It involves instead the presentation of altered social structures. What we are doing is common in the world of management strategy, scientific research and political think tanks. We are involved in the establishment of a series of parallel structures all of which work alongside each other, setting up ways in which it might be possible to understand the complex context within which strategy and the effect of its application is made manifest rather than constantly refining a series of apparently regenerative and predictive statements. When you come across one of our reports it is not necessarily the consolidation of a series of ideas matched up to a network of rational structures, rather the relation between the research and the written work is part of a parallel series of constructions. The reports do not describe various scenarios and scenarios do not illustrate the research. Both work alongside each other. No single element is a complete statement. We are not interested in setting up situations where cause and effect are roughly predictable. Caution is seen as a virtue among political strategists due to developments in psychological research that replaced one stereotype of overly complex compliance with another.

Ramsgate had already stopped listening to himself. Sleeping soundly now, after ten minutes of adjustment and foot rubbing. The video screen forgotten, yet playing late into the afternoon. It would be switched off as the final approach commenced, but there will never be any memory of hitting the red button.

COMPROMISE

In some ways the floor betrayed the age of the building we had come across that day, but it was always hard to tell if the elderly look had been played up or played down. One thing was clear to us though, and that was the extent to which the appearance of a floor like this originated from a historical moment when the structure of a place was to be understood as standing independently of its decoration, from a time when people acknowledged a difference between what a building does and what gets added to it. Lighter in colour, where it had been worn by feet, but also with the potential to be darker in places where frequent passage may not wear surfaces down but add dirt instead. By the large French window that ran from floor to ceiling on the south side of the room, the wood was lighter, the cause of which was not entirely clear. Maybe it was the result of the daily appearance of bright sun through the uneven panes of window glass or it could have been down to the lack of passage through to a rarely accessed area. But then again the space in front of that large floor-to-ceiling window may have witnessed more nervous standing than the rest of the room. Maybe more movement. Maybe less. The windows might have offered access to a frequently used balcony. Unlikely. Consider this. If the house was located in a temperate climate the inconsistent weather might have discouraged frequent use of any balcony, roof garden or terrace. The balcony was to improve the exterior look of the building, not for the beneficial use of its occupants. A temporary conclusion? No a definitive decision. The lighter floor tone close to the window was caused by lack of use. A situation where varnish could not become discoloured and effectively darkened. No excess of access. One way to prove it might have been to lift and fold back the rug that was centred in front of a large purple sofa.

Lincoln is elsewhere, thinking of another plan. Twin seats ranged side by side.

Orange leather bound together by a tubed steel framework. The orange is soft yet stays within roughly squared-off dimensions due to the way it's sewn and stuffed. The frame tubing is chromed to high brightness and cuts slightly into the padded leather. Clearly designed well before this point the seats are locked and caught within the logic of an always-new look. And the walls are brown this time. Chocolate coloured, though not like the surface of a clean fresh slab, more the colour found on the cracked edge when it's snapped in two straight from the fridge. An uneven brown that's both darker and lighter than the face of the industrial poured surface of unwrapped chocolate. So the look of any room is clearer when mediated by Lincoln's thinking. Here's someone certainly far from asleep. The setting up of a think tank about think tanks required a clear mind. A series of statements will be processed in this room. It is a wondering place, and the positioning of the orange chairs is more for a potential audience than the thinker alone. A series of findings will be processed. The think tank about think tanks will be up and running soon. That smashed chocolate wall will frame the analyst and the temporarily absent audience. Sounds familiar, but this situation is not due to haze or vagueness. This think-tank processing place will witness specific work. Let's look at it closely once more. It will help us to understand what may or may not transpire. Aside from the two large orange leather seats there is the possibility to sit in four alternative locations. The set up is convivial, even claustrophobic. Each of the seating possibilities is unique yet related. A sofa, a stool, a bucket chair and a lounger. The materials used to produce the stool and the bucket chair are the same, each being a variation of a set that may also include other furniture, none of which is included in this private place, but it wouldn't take much of a mind leap to see it.

If you were to follow Ramsgate's journey then a visit to that turquoise rental car place would be necessary. A small green car hired and a 85-minute drive east and up. The roads are well-organised and conscientiously maintained, yet they have the typical indirectness of any mountain area. As you go up it is possible to see some highways below, stretching out and gently bending across towards the border area. Houses begin here, evenly spaced, each with substantial land and none of it either pressed into service or overly dressed up in garden style. Ramsgate had taken this trip many times. It used to be a good place to stay. Each house kept apart. Noise played down. No one caring who you were or where you had come from. This part of the country prided itself on tolerance. Curving round a tree-lined portion of black top the road just ends, then a second closer look confirms that it merely drops sharply away right in front of you. But before the drop, take a sharp right and up, change gear, kick down, do something, don't stop but push it. Up and to the right. Then over, and a side sliproad opens out into a roughly oval parking place. Inside the house Ramsgate should be ready. But today there is no car on its way, there never is. Ramsgate is ready all the same. Much older now. Sitting inside. Really awake for the first time. Under a projecting, cantilevered structure. Talking on the telephone. Thinking about building a big conference centre of his own, out here in the mountains.

So let Ron have a go at talking about the place he looks after. The Big Conference Centre back in the city. We can sense that the others are happy to be left alone for a while, the influence of their activity is everywhere, it permeates the fabric of this town. Even The Big Conference Centre is affected. Of course our three could never really be described as being in the background. They are just alongside us, but temporarily out of view and beyond reach.

So Ron, tell us a little bit about this place.

As you may already know, it's a really big conference centre. Our city never got gutted so there was no reason to build it in a dead downtown. Our central area always thrives. So we had no choice but to put the normally regenerative conference centre right out near an airport. Not far from the river, but quite a way from the old centre. I always liked that idea. A centre away from the centre.

All the following things happen at the same time. The second person has decided to set up a think-tank. We see the process of doing this: acquiring a building, employing staff and going through the procedure of working out the best way to communicate findings. The look of the chosen site is described. At the same moment, the first person has decided to take a trip to a series of small islands in the North Atlantic. In search of Discussion Island. The third person is making a section by section breakdown of the index he has been developing. A system waiting for data. Simultaneously the working environment of all three becomes insulated and each one decides that in order to proceed they must work in increasing isolation. They have now entered a post-communication situation. As a post-script to this section the first person creates a précis of the looking-backward syndrome, which is e-mailed to a large number of people. The second and third person are on the list of recipients, but as yet the message goes unread.

Complexity is not an answer. Multiple positioning does, however, allow a strategist to avoid falling into the trap of sidelined research. The cult of self-expression again. Obscurantism is only evident when the wrong structure is applied to the understanding of a series of propositions or statements. Once the restructuring of our work here at the think tank is understood then any potentially obscure elements are clarified.

Do we need a new language to express these ideas? Denmark has a question at last.

This use of the term 'new language' is borrowed from the most dynamic groups in our society, those people at the forefront of establishing new forms of corrected politics. In reality the call for new languages is another 1960s legacy that was absolutely necessary in order to overcome social and political injustice. We know, of course, that languages constantly mutate. We are less interested in apocalyptic linguistic upheavals than we are in the subtle shifts.

Fuzzy sets and parallel occurrences become channelled through specific histories that find old economic models very comforting as places where thinking has been restricted. Possible sites for freethinking parallel today's über-pseudo-global free market economy. Examining a period in British history which spawned the rise of a form of both socialism and modern capitalism. The early nineteenth century and people coming to terms with the recent revolutions in France and America within the context of an emerging system of modern capitalism. Early capitalists from non-conformist religious backgrounds starting to feel guilty, even about Ireland. Becoming interested in a pre-Marxist environment. Drawing parallels between one period and another. The key to this is an interest in temporal shifts through the use of flickering time in relation to the establishment of new think tanks. We have been quite influenced by a younger generation of politicians and their desire to occupy time as much as space without always using television or electronic communication to get their message across.

Lincoln likes to fill up his digital voice.

We were always interested in concepts of freethinking and free will. This is why we spend more and more time expanding. We like a society based on a set of roughly recognisable eighteenth-century European ideas. We have even met dry-cleaners here who believe in free will. We're often interested in reclaiming ideas back away from the form into which they have mutated. The initial impulses that drove the development of social consciousness, have often turned into a form of fetishised individualism where empty signs for individuality replace the real and heartfelt defence of other people's free expression. The examination of older socio-economic models in this context is neither good or bad, it is our obligation to constantly re-examine and take them apart, so we can work out how to use them in a reinvigorated context.

He's warming up, talking to himself, just to make a point.

Failure is at the heart of all utopias. The whole concept of utopia is a Judeo-Christian trap, yet no less seductive for our ability to recognise its origin. Our organisation would argue, however, that the rise of democratic socialism was beyond utopian, in the sense that it either tried to stun people out of the hypnotic belief in the potential of tomorrow or tried to build a better situation right here and right now. So whether you are looking at pre-war housing projects in Rotterdam on the one hand or the reconfigured politics of identity on the other, both key realignments were attempting to go beyond utopic fantasy. So I would say that we are not involved in an ongoing disaster, instead it is necessary to recognise the fact that the socio-political hierarchies that we used to be addressing have multiplied and changed. Classic twentieth-century western social theory was not dislocated or disenfranchised, to abandon it all in favour of an ironic position now is to misunderstand what postmodern analysis was about. The sun sets fast in this part of the country. From the mountain house it'll go quick, shaded behind the mass of rock to the west.

NEGOTIATION

Supposing that the rug had been in the same place for any length of time, which we were not in a position to assume, it might be possible to ascertain the use and ageing pattern of the floor based upon the condition of a little used or essentially protected portion of it that lay underneath. The rug could have been called a carpet. No one can remember how big it was. Placed squarely on the wooden floor, predominantly light brown and black. The layering of the single rug on the wooden planked floor backed up the feeling that someone had encouraged a sense of age at ground level. Old carpet, old floor. Solidity and authenticity underfoot. The rug had no fringe around its perimeter and was greatly worn. So thin, almost like looking at the back of fine cloth. The weave and the pattern were integrated. With the thinness and the integration it was possible to lay it down either way up. Except that right here the pattern would suffer from alterations, even reversal moments at meeting points between the two or three different types of yarn, that would render it out of sync with the rest of the room. The pattern was simple but just sufficiently complex to avoid rapid visual possession. A pattern just loaded enough to indicate that it was a pattern rather than a series of simple shapes. Just. Twenty seconds of looking would have revealed that we were faced with a small number of decorative devices combined in a familiar order to create a floor covering both vaguely disorientating and immediately negotiable with little further thought. A floor, a rug, some age over-stated.

The stool and the chair are constructed from a complex of thin metal rods. In the case of the stool the rods are gently curved. From a wide base diameter they swing inwards for about two thirds of their length and then outwards again to provide enough circumference to offer support for a padded top. The top is brown. Almost a direct match for that one brown tone used on the framing wall. The seat cushion is gently curved and padded yet not to an extreme. The top looks like it could be firm. The chair uses the same large number of rods as the stool, probably chromed. Yet in this case they all slope inwards from the supporting diameter towards a smaller area of engagement with the seat. Only at this point do they slope out sharply and curve up to form a back and side support, the rods at the front stopping short and neatly finishing with a single line that creates a shallow u-shape in order to frame the front and arm sides of the chair. Such an arrangement would offer some support up to the middle back of any sitter, and then little else. The top of the back rest and arm support is completed in the same material as the seat of the stool and chair. A tapering pad of brown that is highest at the back and moves gently towards the armrest ends. The effect of the rod bases is primarily optical. Any light shifts through these structures, destabilised and fluid. Yet the seats also appear lightweight and strong. Specifically made yet not authored enough to ensure total memory. Trophy chairs. Expensive and dated, the sofa brown, on the other hand, has some white within the weave. The white alters the light in a different way. Same colour, different tone. It is gently curved all over, but unlike the chair and stool keeps an essentially squared off shape. The lounger in the corner is made of leather and metal. Twentieth-century furniture options. A long, flat and gently curved slab of black leather forms a seating pad. A second, squarer slab forms the back rest.

Sitting, a little startled. For the first time in years having made a call rather than receiving one. Speaking about something quite central to a developing conception of action and activity. That is, a slow and methodical version of events. It had been a long journey before this sojourn. Nearly a year away looking for that special island. Now a temporary conclusion had been reached. At least ten different locations could pass as the site for parallel work. Sitting here under a platform, working the telephone. Listening more than speaking. Looking up and to the side. In the borderless garden some birds are hopping and some know how to walk. A key to small differences of intelligence. Small chipmunks are dipping and nodding. Capable of clambering fast onto the twined ball of a bushy shrub without falling through light twigs to the ground. Constantly hungry, everything living and always feeding. Ramsgate listening hard. Looking up and then to the side. Wondering where a chipmunk would sleep at night. Nodding. Stupid, distracting questions. Not pressing enough to require answers. All the deals are falling into some kind of place. Negotiations of ownership are not the issue with these islands. It's more a question of sneaky use and how to get around difficulty of access. Pull away from this scene and see that first person clearly, sitting cross-legged on the floor, projected upon and glowing with multiple shadows.

Anyway they got together and provided some money raised from a whole diverse bunch of people and organisations. We're not really a city that anyone thought needed something like this. But now it's here I suppose it performs a useful function. It's certainly popular. Thousands come from all over the world to meet each other, listen and present. Sometimes it's clear that most of the process is elaborated towards a simple engagement. Just to walk around in a smiley daze waiting for meeting and exchange. We never really noticed the need for this place. It just crept up on all of us. Me? I'm quite happy with it. Providing a serious job and money. Within this kind of structure no one really knows the value or meaning of any specific job description, so there's not the same kind of potential humiliation through relative employment status. We are very creative with our job titles. You are foolish to imagine that we would be embarrassed by the service-orientated nature of what we do. If things get too complicated then we just change our job titles, have endless meetings and even conferences on the renaming and readjustment of our activities.

Our attention flickers between the three people as they each encounter a situation with a different projecting platform under which an exchange takes place. Discussion, negotiation, delay. Each person leaves the platform locations. All three pass the same insulation plate. Ramsgate begins work on an illustrated scenario. Lincoln attempts to come up with a written language that can be replicated and understood by as many people as possible. Each person receives a special gift that echoes and amplifies their process of communication. Of course, each present takes a different form. Ramsgate goes on a journey north through areas of industrial decay. At a small village he goes to see someone. That night Ramsgate dreams of think-tank systems. We follow each of them as they go about their daily business, they are temporarily involved now in supplying basic foods, materials and services. We rapidly move to Lincoln who is hosting a seminar around the idea of creating an assessment tank that will permit constant ongoing critique of the near future. It is a fine summer morning. Denmark is sitting in a small summerhouse, working on a section by section breakdown of research strategies in western-European nations. We see the beauty of the countryside and we follow as he takes a trip through this landscape with a group of small children. They reach a place in the woods where they sit under a platform and argue. In mid-flow Denmark realises that the issue of negotiation is not merely restricted to the sponsorship of exchange but can depend on personal focus. So he concentrates hard for a moment upon the possible development of those children. We see Ramsgate, Lincoln and Denmark going through an elaborate series of arrivals and departures in many different situations and many different countries. At least five years pass and all we witness are comings and goings.

Denmark is a house guest. Visiting for more than the weekend.

He's relaxed and entertaining.

I remember having a dinner with a French strategist and an American newspaper editor and the editor asked the strategist what the politics were of a little known French postmodernist theorist. The strategist did not understand the question, because of course the theorist was a Marxist. The magazine editor did not understand how the theorist could be a Marxist when his writing appeared to be so lacking in old-school moral judgement and so potentially useful for 'the wrong side' in a constantly mutating capitalist context. This issue of adaptability being the best indicator of success is a form of economic Darwinism gone crazy. The host thinks that Denmark is funny but wrong. Further down the table someone changes the subject. Our work is based upon an exploitation of parallel structures. As a result it is often a mistake to look across from one stream of research to another. The stuff that leaks out fulfils certain functions that authorised results cannot easily cope with. This is not to privilege dissent, but to acknowledge different speeds and even temperatures of communication. We are very interested in the idea of our reports being provisional. The idea of potential as a dominant indicator of viability while working towards a series of concepts seems much more radical to us than the distilled, concluded research. The alternative for some time has been documentary structures created by outsiders, but they tend to create situations in our organisation where the intentions and results of the researcher appear to become too even and pedantic. Showing and telling in place of a matrix.

Our ambiguous relation to any report and to its history is an aspect of our ability to be a site for future thinking. Each of our constructions is prototypical and provisional. Denmark, no longer trusts himself with other people's research and recognises the fuzzy border zones between one set of ideas and another. No one will notice, at least in the short term.

A question for Lincoln. Is the clarity and clean modern look of your office an antidote to the clatter of your ideas or the echo of an image-packed world? People turned to a lack of complexity as a location of profound thought in the west as part of the general influence of Zen-modernism. Lincoln is speaking. Despite all Ramsgate's claims, people still used his primary research as something to zone out to. Our office is a reversal of The Big Conference Centre model. In that scenario the design works as the base level for activity. The flexibility of the building becomes a parallel visualisation of the potential framing of ideas in a generalised sense. Within our new office, we wanted to play with certain concepts and return to the question of how to project an image, the way in which we are held in the thrall of promise and potential made manifest, and combined with a look at the idea of the centre ground of socio-economic organisation from corporate stress to bureaucratic compromise. Initially we attempted to repeat ourselves and create a large unwieldy building, getting around the question "Where are you located?" by creating a series of concentrated core sites instead. Yet when attempting to address the near future, the classic postmodernist game of multiplied research was not possible so we had to create core sites first. To do so resulted in an illusion of projection. Recognising the fact that it might be possible to take some of our prototypical thinking and to develop it further, in order to address certain ideas from the centre of action and predictive thinking, we understood that we had to think hard about the look of our offices. So we kept what we had already got and installed overhead platforms and related screens that could project a space, where it might be possible to consider key issues before too much research had taken place. The building really works alongside the research. It is not emptied out because no one is expected to fill up some notional void with complex presentation, instead it might be possible for our office to act as a backdrop within which a series of scenarios may be played out. We are no longer dealing with furniture meets thought, the relationship is less functional and strangely brittle. A constant flickering of idea, intention and potential towards an excess of access and a reclamation of the middle ground. Permission to play out some vague scenarios within a visual context that mashes design and dogma.

A big silver car arrives and disappears into an underground car park.

DELAY

So imagine walking into a room with Coca-Cola coloured walls. Sitting there for quite a time. Noticing little of the interior beyond an overdose of flooring. The continuing sequence of events must have started and then spun off from this place. Seven-Up coloured curtains? The first person had been dreaming, half asleep and half awake. Ramsgate. No remembering, but a mesh of forward and therefore by association, backward thinking. Recently it had become clear that there might be a necessity to go beyond the kind of physical sensation described by Ramsgate's brain. A need-to-know base for spin-off activity. A time to look forward into the not-too-distant future. To play with projection. The establishment of tomorrowism. A simple process had been underway. Three people are now considering the possibility of writing this report, each under-developed in terms of scope and mood. Ramsgate, Lincoln and Denmark, shifting quickly around through varied landscapes. Each of them up to something. All frequently bounding right past each other. A global matrix of action will be playing out just in front of us. Two minutes or two days away. Never clear, but at least we have established the base of a building from which to develop various possibilities as they come to us. A first person, Ramsgate. A second, Lincoln and the third, Denmark. Constantly shifting, all negotiating the soon-to-take-place. Each trying to reassess the potential of projection. Looking at issues in the centre ground from alongside. Middled and mobile. All capable of reaching beyond the moment, but only just. "If only it could be better tomorrow!" Enough thrall. Looking at the pattern into which social behaviour and economic systems naturally fall and realising that it takes some effort to maintain that illusion.

Move up rapidly now to a window. Straight through and inside. The furniture remains specific.

That whole thing in the corner is like a chair that has been stretched out and turned into a simple variant of something much better. Like a seating unit rather than a chair. Yet Ramsgate's ability to judge the relative success or failure of that other chair is based on memory rather than photographs. It is quite possible that all variants of this chair are wrong. None quite interesting enough to firmly lodge in the mind. A room. Predominance of brown. A thinking place. That's clear. With too many chairs so nowhere to sit. Each time the think-tank thinker went inside it was necessary to wonder aloud where to crash. Lincoln, lie down on that sofa. Lincoln, sit in the orange and be your own audience. Lincoln perches on a stool. Lincoln, recline on the stretched-out leather or use the bucket. I know. Just stand there for a second. No. No thinking can take place for a few minutes, then action, slow and methodical action. Yes shift the orange leather. It's heavy, they're both heavy. They weigh a ton. Hang on, just put the papers down. Elsewhere in the building people have started working. Compiling lists and information on all the other think tanks they can find. All sense of projection is being collated. Papers are being asked for and organised into trend-based parallels. Put them down, stupid. The papers, stupid, push all the dumb objects that cover the folded Plexi coffee tables onto the floor. There you go. A nice noise. Things have been too controlled. This is Lincoln's private room. Things can get clunky here. The ashtray, moulded and pewtered. Another in ceramic. Nice and heavy. Each falls along with those yellow buds sitting in their aluminium tubes. Worst of all the knotted glass thing that people always used to comment on. At least they did when they ever came here. No recent visitors. All onto the floor but no clanking, silenced by heavy carpeting.

Five years. A city centre is rebuilt. New hotels. Some children and a major ring road.

Walking through an enormous city, Lincoln had just had lunch. Not a bad day. Some interesting developments in terms of the key to current think-tank structuring. An important meeting with a person who had the longest list of groups currently in the process of development and soon-to-be aiding projection. For the last five years the compilation of working processes and findings had expanded considerably. True, finding a way to work through all the stuff had become problematic, but at the moment those earlier complications made little difference. High as a kite again. Turned on by all this centre ground modelling combined with the creation and application of various scenarios. "What's it going to be like tomorrow?" "Well, how would you like it to be?" Lincoln stepped neatly aside to avoid crashing into a tall person and laughed. Pausing now for a second. Looking up and to the side. Reaching out from a concrete building. A projected place. Somewhere to stand and think for a moment. A negotiation will have to happen. Some people are closing in. No way can Lincoln go forward without getting past some structural problems. Stand aside again. Wait and think. Things are not really going that smoothly. The mass of information is not helping, it's holding everything back. Stand and think for a minute or two longer, out here in the street. Up above the air conditioning drips. Water drops onto the canopy. OK. Here it is. After some time the necessity arose to develop organisations that could create more and more sophisticated models for what might take place. All in order to continue a form of development and potential. Yet that process of prediction in turn altered the way source material, research, could be understood. Behaviour influenced by the knowledge that it would be watched, assessed and reworked. Examine the tanks themselves and you might get beyond this thinking. Watch them all. Monitoring. Yes of course, a form of monitoring. Watching the watchers, check to see how those searches for a middle way encourage a form of centrism that holds us into short term steps. A concentration upon all who watch rather than looking constantly at the source. That's the idea. Negotiate the negotiators. Denmark too is under a platform. Held up. Not able to move. Enough to make anyone go crazy.

Back five years ago. Up in the conference centre.

But Ron, we know all of this. No emotion will ever stir our trio. Why not speak of the place itself? I know, describe your favourite room.

Up, right at the top, over on the side furthest from the river, there's a room here that overlooks a wide highway. I like the way that the whole place is designed. The building somehow spans the road. Sky-walks criss-cross the expanse of pale concrete as it swoops below. So the highway and that side of the building have been integrated. The strange thing about it though, is that you can't see the highway from this room. You can't even hear it. But I know that it's there. One of my greatest pleasures is to be in this room during some kind of event. Knowing that the highway is 200 feet below, yet nobody can see or hear it. The room was set aside when the designers of this place realised that if they were to install the decorative atrium they all desired, and taking into account the peculiar shape of the air-conditioning system, which had been substituted for the first choice soon after construction began on the realisation that the original wouldn't pump out sufficient freshened air for the whole place. Hold it Ron.

We sense the presence of the three people at work at every moment, yet their influence is only in the background for a while, and instead we see the way certain urban structures have developed. Five years later, our out-of-focus view pulls into a clearer, slower, series of images. We notice only the differences that have been wrought over the intervening period. Ramsgate is playing a game. Lincoln is creating a series of complex tasks for a number of other people, while Denmark establishes a complex database that works to anticipate and thereby accentuate progression and change for an individual's own benefit. Think-tank systems are used to monitor these developments. And at a crucial moment each person has to compromise and set up a parallel way of working instead of maintaining the illusion of ploughing onwards.

Denmark is facing a room full of people.

In order to understand the way this report has developed it is crucial to realise that the relationships between the research and the conclusions is of a different order to that which we have developed in previous years. One of the key things to understand is that we are not dealing with a traditional resolution of intuition and data. In recent projects a research base was used as a concentrated core from which a number of potential scenarios could spring. In direct response to that way of working came the examination of ideas located in the middle ground. Increasing curiosity about the notion of projection as a central support for the development of our situation. The way thinking about the future changes the future and how reflecting upon the past alters our perception of what has taken place. And the extent to which such thinking has been glossed over by projection alone. Initially we used the same technique that we had found so useful in the past. A focus upon this idea of a concentrated core of research material towards the development of a number of scenarios. It soon became clear to us, however, that applying this process to the idea of how to think about the future only leads to corruption. In an effort to grasp a sense of the potential fluidity of the middle ground we realised it would be a good idea to develop some new physical settings and situations before embarking on the report stage. These precise locations could then change the mood of those working on the report. Their input to their environment could begin to pre-empt the complexity of the work ahead.

Everything has potential use in our scenarios. Whether you offer an analysis of flower production or information about immigration in Belgium. Both these things would have a potential that is understandable and linked to a combination of things like the intention of the report author, their intelligence and their ability to communicate. Our recent research is no more complex than gathering data towards the creation of a series of scenarios that are concerned with apparently secondary social components. Not fundamental questions but connected to communication, discussion, negotiation and compromise as autonomous concepts. Maybe in the past people were locked out of development. Now it is essential to allow a period of general response, some space where things open up before a report can be concluded. It is no accident therefore that this Big Conference Centre is attractive. Bright colours, aluminium, light and design. We are actively trying to lure people, elicit an interim response rather than provide one. And the process seems to have worked. To a certain extent we have gathered more ideas this way, from quite surprising sources, than if we had presented our findings as a conclusion to a specialised set of thinkers. It is both pleasurable and disconcerting for us to hear words like beautiful in relation to something that we have spent so much care to embody with a sense of generic utility. Not because we don't like beautiful places, but because we have maybe come up with a new form of elegant utility.

Reframing and reinterpretation. First there is an attractive, even beautiful place, later a report is written.

When you have a set of ideas there are many ways to communicate them. Tomorrow is often a question of what not to do rather than what to do. We are always interested to occupy those small gaps between social effects. We are not so interested to reinforce our work as separate from all those activities that are close to it. On the other hand we remain suspicious of people who claim that the introduction of the look of revolt is enough to create some effect. So we are constantly trying to remain in our border zone. We want to look at an idea as complex as how we think about the very near future, so in a post-utopian environment we have to be careful not to over determine research before we begin. Most think-tank activity is a functional way to avoid having to invent minor details in some bigger story. Research is validation. There is another thing to be conscious of and that is the way the image of this organisation will be altered by the content of the report that is yet to be written. The think-tank scenarios currently under development are not mute or ironic markers of our time but remain flexible, tied to other findings and to a mess of contradictory possibilities. If they were conclusions, or the end of a set of thinking, they would fail. There is a provisional quality to the process and that is important for us, we invite people to be involved in the intellectual reframing of the conclusion, we don't present something and then ask everyone to try and work out the solution to the scenario. If you can't stand in the way of progress, maybe we can hinder development.

CONSENSUS

Lying down in a place that might have once held a bed but now only offered some soft dented furniture. Thin eyes closed yet the face betraying a degree of consciousness that couldn't exactly be described as sleeping, couldn't really be called awake. No need to ask yourself what was going on here. A person alone in a room with Coca-Cola coloured walls. Dark hair and blue clothing. Shoes abandoned by a cream door. Socked feet occasionally rubbing together. Thinking about a number of objects and images from the recent past. The list is of the type that goes on and on. So here we are with just a beginning of the inventory. A panel is over Ramsgate's head, screens side by side. Some things work better in the background. Panelling. Bare metal that conceals and protects. Lighting has been thought through extremely carefully. Everything here can be assessed most effectively at the point where ideas and actions meet. Caught in the centre ground. Conciliation teams up with compromise. More things. Some components, shielded and prototypical. The kind of look that prompts slipping thoughts. We can sit watching the half sleeper, half awaker and begin to list the issues played out around those objects. The every-day things that refer to a collective sense of tomorrow. Conciliation, compromise, arrival, delay, negotiation, reconciliation, platforms, consensus, dialogue, retribution, liability, resignation, concentration, decision, assessment, revision, flow, consultation, reconsideration. There will be more listing after this. 1971/1985/1998, specific dates of significance that require extra examination. The years before key events. It is necessary for Ramsgate to try and develop some ideas, understand why it happens to be the moment to visualise via projection from the centre. Creating an avoidance of technology while at the same time side-stepping a cult rooted in research of apparently authentic behaviour. Thinking aloud while remaining in this half-coma. Just starting to consider the way things might be yet always restricting vision. A repossession of the not-too-distant future. Time to get out of the room.

Walking now in the street there are elements of the situation and the environment that are recognisable. A kind of city has been dressed in urban drab. The look is deliberate and has been enforced. Back in the room Ramsgate stays still, but thoughts are wandering again. Each place has been added to, but every addition is beyond fundamental and involves some protection of the space. A series of surface covers. Projecting places beneath which it might be possible to consider the potential of tomorrow. It will always be necessary to make sure that some of the stuff remains the same. There must always be something to compare. A physical, environmental control. Background context, reassuring and precise. It could all be cleared away right now, but that would leave a clean slate. All of these elements will be described later. Time to speed up a little. Ramsgate is about to snap out of it.

Throw the tables out the window. No one knows if there is a balcony or not. Shift the stool, the bucket chair and push those orange leather lumps. But without the weight of the other furniture on the rug any attempt to push means the chairs catch and snag. Ah, the rug. That's the focus of this second person. An opportunity to stretch out on the floor. It's the best. So furry. Shagged close to Afghan. Artificial, yet made from wool. Woolly mammoth. Fur carefully made, not skinned. So that's why we heard nothing when things were slid off the Plexi tables. Everything is neatly cushioned here. You could sit on the stool and learn to juggle eggs. Even the most hopeless beginner could make a start at it. Each time an egg dropped it would be carefully held in the fluff. So the big leather chairs will have to be lifted. From behind. Take them from behind. Hump up. Stagger back and away, tiny steps Lincoln, each testament to the strain involved, but it's worth it. Now down on the floor, everything is clear enough down there. Fall forwards onto knees and hands, crawl along and bury your face in the rug. Stay that way for a moment. Rest comes easily once the chairs are shifted. But up too quick again. Light-headed, stars burning blue and pink in the eyes. Little floaters showing up on the lens with the sudden brightness of this private place. Where are the papers? Enough preparation. It's time to look things over properly and for the first time. One. Two. Three. Walk away.

Leaving the protection of the projection. Some progress is being made. It's raining, it's snowing and it's changeable. Three separate locations all quite apart from each other. As each walks away there's a simultaneous look to the left. One attracted by a noise, Lincoln catching a colour flash in the corner of the eye and Denmark feeling a physical pull to the right. There, on the side of a building is a large solid plate of metal. It protects and insulates. Immediate recognition of the function of that plate is not possible. But it is a sign for all three. Something to look out for in the not-so-distant future. None of them ever imagined that they were really alone in this work. But now it is becoming clear that other people have been this way before and they were stopped. Halted. OK, not in such a precise way. But there is some evidence that they were hindered in an organised fashion.

So they were left with space turned into an enormous tribute to flexibility. Somewhere not planned but perfect as a location to excel. A structure within an over-planned place that could be completed without regard to function. Almost as if the people who designed The Big Conference Centre were looking for an opportunity to fuck up. Not because they were bad architects or planners, just that there was an unspoken agreement not to notice this overlooked floor. It is unbelievable that it could have been passed through so many meetings and countless revisions unnoticed. Yet oversights happen and they happen deliberately. The only answer to why we were left with an enormous empty room is that people chose not to notice that low but expansive area. They all wanted it to be ignored during the allocation of functions so they all pretended not to see it. Knowing that it wouldn't be accepted by anyone, the room became a tribute to amnesia. They conspired in pursuit of flexibility. Not being stupid they all knew that a place like this needs something extra. With that Big Conference Centre, if you planned it, filled it, designated it and located it then there would have been no room for the kind of realisations that come with changing minds and wilful design for its own sake. They all wanted a room that represented the aspirations of the building. It couldn't be planned into the development so it was willed into existence instead.

We are entering a moment of digression where it is necessary to tell three stories. Each character is in a different location. One is at home in a big modern house, the second is lost in a European city, moving from bar to bar and the third is at a seminar to discuss the potential of managing ecological crisis and ways to profit from it. The first person relates a story to an extended family about a desire to recreate the life of a lone yachtsman who cheated in a round the world race many years earlier. The second person tells a story of an army captain who walked to Siberia alone and in his regular city clothing. The third person bemoans the decline in the production of predictive reports. Each of the three goes into a situation where they can be alone for a second and they each come across the same book. We have no idea what this book is. The first person has to answer a telephone call. The second person finds a hotel and writes a letter and the third person is grabbed and taken out by an old close friend. Each of them tells a tale of business fantasy and control systems, the three are now in sync and each can begin or end each other's statements. They are working.

One could get the idea that as a think tank, we are focusing on narrative structures and claiming a stake in the future. That means our presentations, no matter what they look like, try to initiate different possibilities of reading. In regards to the perception of our research as a reading process we can define the difference between aspects of information, indexing and reporting.

A plane flies overhead. A blue shape is painted onto the rear tail fin.

There is a sense in which we are trying to cover many aspects of negotiation. We always felt uncomfortable with the way in which political strategists were pressured to resolve their work into an illusion of precise limited concerns in order to indicate vision and drive. As an organisation we are not so interested in the serial production of reports and statements, which for us make a point about the speed of modern communication that we feel is redundant. The way capitalism works is dynamic and fluid. The rules are constantly being rewritten and the aims redefined. We want to reclaim such an area of fluidity into mutating micro-conclusions that might include elements of the poetic, the informational and purely strategic but all of this is framed by a constant play between activity and analysis. Strategists are also told that their role is to find an easy way to communicate in a complex environment and therefore they have an obligation to overstate their ideas through repetition and refinement. We think that the idea of communication and information transferral is important but our reports should not be relegated to the status of an overplayed reminder of the tiny shifts possible with the illusion of constant values, even if those constants are a repeated message about how it is no longer possible to be sure about anything. We are interested in issues of time without necessarily relating today and tomorrow. There is only the possibility to create a fragmented understanding of our work, an issue we are aware of and constantly try to manipulate. No one can ever grasp the immensity of our task.

The audience offers polite acknowledgement of a disordered mind.

We can always tell you something about being involved in the intellectual reframing of ideas. It is important for us to involve other organisations as co-authors.

Outside a dog walks a meandering course to the river.

At this moment it is important for us to expose ourselves to potentially discordant, even contradictory, conclusions. We have already reached the point where we have presented all the data that we need to set a number of scenes. Think tanks are given permission by the rest of us to investigate the small spaces and fuzzy border areas that create the dynamic swings of focus between activities. Projects like ours cannot go any further without regular brainstorming sessions. We will be offering a series of presentations that reveal the potential of developing a post-predictive report.

A programme of public and private meetings that will yield results regardless of what takes place. But this is not an interactive process in the normal sense of the term. There is no pressure on others to come to terms with our thinking. If people want to come and witness an organisation get their concepts in a twist then that's fine with us. They can just act as observers. This is also a genuine invitation to get involved with the complications of how to think ahead. To reposition the work of an organisation involved in the predictive process within a broader web of action and reflection. Of course, other people are always involved in our activities, it is just that this time the nature of that involvement is transparent and acknowledged.

A boat moves from side to side while a dog sniffs a ball of paper.

Our presentations always function on multiple levels. First there is an outline, a kind of introduction into the basic ideas which require addressing. Next, a first meeting with people from within our organisation who are interested in contributing to the project. Later on a report is published. Our working technique splits up and consists of many equivalent parts, all of which form a broad and ever-expanding final stage that feeds into subsequent projects. Compared to a lot of think tanks our technique might appear strange. Many users of our predictions expect a single conclusive report and find the entry point to the research is mutable.

A car crashes alone into a country ditch. The driver drips blood onto his broken hands.

It is important for us to offer different levels of access to our work. It should be possible to enter at any point. Yet there is some desire to acknowledge the web of contradictions and desires that exist in constant flux around any particular moment of thinking ahead. It would not be enough to only present process projects in every situation as it would also be insufficient to engage in interactive situations alone. We are not convinced that our work particularly privileges structure above anything else, but maybe the potential access to a web of surrounding self-generating context is what makes structural concerns appear important. There are many situations where we present singular conclusions, but the function of such interim findings often shifts. We alter the point in any set of thinking from which we might choose to spin off with something to present to a broader audience. We are not always looking at the end point alone because we cannot see a beginning either. We think it is this technique which leads to the idea that structure is so important. We would prefer to see our working process as connected with a necessity to constantly redefine the points when micro-conclusion become significant and to spread them across any given time period rather than saving them up for an end. The process has always already begun. We are not interested in defining origins or end points. These are desires that arose this century, leading to the increasing dislocation of projection. Everything feeds off itself. There is no logical self-supporting structure, merely occasional decisions to pull out something in order to proceed. A couple of years ago we presented a series of reports in relation to the unification of western-European aspirations. We constructed a large set and placed copies of the various reports on a table alongside a number of raw data files. A British economist offered us his understanding of the reports, suggesting that it might be necessary to read all the data in order to comprehend all the reports. Obviously on one level you don't need reports to comprehend data but on the other hand if you really want to know about projection an infinite number of reports would never be enough. Our point is that the economist remained committed to understanding the data as the source towards a resolved unity of ideas rather than acknowledging the potential of layering and various temperatures of communication in the final reports. If anything our work is anti-structural in the sense that there is no unitary logic to all the elements of a particular project. At all times elements spin off and affect the reading of the research and vice versa. Our interest in time and the middle ground ensures that hierarchies are corrupted but not suppressed into useless structural equivalence.

A young man accidentally blows himself up into smallish

snotty pieces inside a coal shed. He sees the flash and arms and legs crumple in the first stages of a searing blast.

REVISION

Ramsgate remembered trying to put together an argument. Each time confronted by the need to explain, contradicted by a requirement to know more, caught within a technique that relied upon identifying whoever might be the best at indicating and exposing the kind of action that proved the existence of pivotal moments. That old key-moment syndrome. Whoever it might be that could take on the recent past and combine it most effectively with an illusion of the near future. Basically trying to get hold of, and then express, an understanding of mediation rather than original action. Where the potential of the near future is already in existence, looking for the shift, not the source. As Ramsgate was always happy to point out, in that half-asleep and half-awake state, the strategic mobility of dominant systems had already been consolidated. Other people are hyper-pivotal. In fact what was taking place with such pivot persons was a reconciliation of the past with the present. Not coping with issues of projection at all. In a constant state of looking for the turning points. The only way through for that first person was to find a way to address the centre without resorting to the fetish of the pivotal but also without falling into the trap of looming off to revive and reinvent the past. The issue here is of how to squirm free, wake up and resist the thrall of tomorrowism, and instead to address the issue of who controls prediction. At least it seems that way for our half awaker. Thinking away, Ramsgate knows the task ahead. For the others, knowing the pivotal moments is still the key. They found it exciting and still do. But for the sleeper, such thinking links up to a whole set of moral and ethical superstitions. Forget the symbols and try to grasp the day-to-day process of decision making.

Staff are to be employed and will be going through the procedure of working out the best way to communicate. Let's not go into it. They will talk and talk. Working from a distance is not an option this time.

That stuff about simultaneous discoveries based on singular research. There can be no flashing or flickering here. Everything functioning in parallel. Back to Ramsgate.

Number one has decided to take a trip to a series of small islands in the North Atlantic. A long deferred trip in search of Discussion Island. A place to work out some centre ground ideas. They existed, it existed, that location for reconciliation. The fantasy of collective minds operating in a pre-twentieth-century environment. These people alone are not responsible for creating the myth, merely reinforcing it. Discussion Island. A place which bears no trace of volcanic activity or glacial scars. Near to Ireland, Iceland, Greenland. In a smaller sea maybe. Intimate beyond the green black of North Atlantic passage. A peninsula blocks off sight. Nothing is clear. One solution is a staked claim to a number of sites. Lincoln will have access to enough resources. Enabling a little corner to be had in each of numerous potential places. Who cares if none are that older Discussion Island, they are all close enough. Each can become a staging post towards further examination, places where it might be possible to model the effects of negotiation. Searches will definitely happen. The best sites located. All Discussion Islands will be named and opened up, each kept in Lincoln's control for now. Some disastrous dreaming will be involved along the way. Operating as sites beyond talk, each will have to be looked after by a vast staff. It's hopeless to try and understand all of Lincoln's motives. But let's allow indulgence. A way to think about the implications of tomorrow without resorting to edgy technology. An expensive rebuilding of a series of locations, none of which will necessarily fulfil all the conditions needed to grasp the potential of tomorrow. The potential of potential.

Ramsgate was on the telephone for a reason. Talking in order to visualise. A series of illustrations are required for a strategist such as this. The semi sleeper needs a way to picture some scenarios. Each story line can be put into images. A series of closely-organised graphics that will aid an understanding of any situation regardless of details, so on the phone again, conjuring up images of compromise, conciliation, delay. Creating the possibility of putting together an effective operational platform based on pictures. At the same time Lincoln has realised the necessity to alter the linguistic structure applied so far to all that work in search of Discussion Island. Naomccolloola. New language enough. Take hold of the technical words, then translate everything into that refreshed conceptual core. More mobile in terms of understanding. An increase in the number of terms with which to address the addressees. The creation of a coded, yet highly effective language. Not so difficult to imagine, more like a redesign. Refurbishment of the key phrases. Just because something takes so long to develop doesn't mean that it is the only way to put together some type of language. In any case we only have to deal with writing, not speaking. Lincoln needs a way to communicate faster across existing linguistic barriers. So that new language will speed things up. Super fast. That's the point. There might now be time to get through what needs to be achieved, at least for one third of this report. The hope is that everyone will be able to understand. And no one is really sure that Lincoln has factored that into his constipated equation. New languages bring a different order of problems.

That's my favourite room. And right now it looks like the only properly planned space in the place. If only you could make time to get all the way up the building. My favourite room now seems so specialised. As if it was the only truly designed part of this compromised architecture. Extreme, yet the result of negotiation. Care got lavished here as soon as the collective architectural group committed to revealing the room's location and even admitting to conversation about its potential. The hyperbole in front of the cladding. Each knew that the creation of a crisis and a series of problems would aid the possibility of spending some money here. Remember this is a portion of The Big Conference Centre. If it was ignored for long enough, the best chamber would become a problem. Difficulties need rapid negotiation. And each planner here knuckled under with the challenge. And of course the possibility to resolve the crisis was given to the best The top-notch interior person knew that such a recently revealed and embarrassingly empty, unnoticed space would be given to the group. I knew in my heart that this top person had been the first one to begin ignoring the space. Hoping beyond hope. And then knowing for sure that it would always be bypassed and unseen as long as the top planner appeared not to notice. Such an opportunity for development through negligence, gave solace to everyone who believed in the power of the blind eye.

This part exists in the form of a memo/e-mail drafted by all three to each other, addressing in different ways certain structural issues: 1) The way to come to decisions. 2) A negotiation of presentation tools. 3) An effective operational process of ongoing micro-conclusion and constant revision. The first person has a powerful sexual experience. The second person is beaten up and the third person attempts to fly.

So were people this dumb before television?

Lincoln turned and smiled.

Video and television are the only areas where strategists still worry about technique and style of presentation. And they feel excluded. Many of them are concerned with television as a physical presence in a person's house and they don't really play with what's shown on it. There is the idea that once access has been gained the message will inevitably get across. Political strategists think they can do something clever with television because television is clever as a medium. We don't think people have changed much, however we have found that television has encouraged a new kind of strategic dumbness on the part of strategists in relation to manipulation and analysis.

Thank you for coming this afternoon. Firstly, the use of global networks, simultaneously avoiding ongoing reports of micro-conclusion. Second, research material combined with interim findings. I'm sure that you agree that this would appear to have some appeal. We must allow for instant response. Our organisation understands general tendencies and we're quite sympathetic to most of them. We like control systems that use cinematic techniques derived from data analysis. We can understand why other people would like that too, it goes along with earlier democratised ideas of information transferral. What we're more confused about is why people don't get think tanks set up in their own organisations. Why did think tanks not become a real personal statement? When we set one up for our domestic pleasure, we went to a house and just used it to analyse TV with. It was really amazing. You watch a normal afternoon game show on the ceiling with constant analysis alongside and it's a real improvement.

We are faced with a separation of the professional and the domestic that was encouraged by electronics companies. It goes along with a fetish of technology. At the beginning we were very good at bringing the professional into the domestic. Tape recording, for example, only existed in the professional field during the 1940s, and people did not really know what they could use it for in everyday life. We blurred the professional and the domestic. Made both areas disappear, sucked into each other. Yet other companies have lost this adaptability. Marketing analysis led to a recognition that people enjoyed the idea that they could professionalise that domestic environment and vice versa. The way think-tank tools are used now ensures that they remain in the professional sphere of distanced interrogation while masquerading as an open forum. We can't believe we're talking about digital potential, but the point is simple. We're losing our position through deliberate loss of control.

Pulling ourselves together for a moment, after all there is an audience here.

Well for our most recent research we were thinking of using frequently mutating digital conferencing devices but we finally decided to use a closed 'one-to-one' technology. We're not particularly interested in digital graphical interfaces, and some of our sources are still interrogated in open conference, face-to-face, which is a definitively anachronistic set up, but we love it. We don't care about this fascination for technology for its own sake.

Slowly, extremely slowly, a stream of water starts to fill up the basement.

What we're actually trying to do with this project, and it's something which is really a typical example of the way that a lot of work we do is kind of out of balance, is try to destabilise something right at the moment when it's becoming fixed within a politicised discourse. We're always very interested in questions of self-created context, the way people play with how their activities are monitored. Our documentation represents documentation, yet raw data alone is not a very effective information carrier. The essential thing is our unique combination of transparent research and multiple findings, constantly adjusted and open to compromise. Documentaries are normally seen at the endpoint and are fragmented images from a series of progressions. We work backwards towards the fundamental impressions that frame our research. It's a kind of semantic game, but it's not just about production strategies, although there is some strategic play as well. Oh, and yes, lots of recognisable references are made to things in the arena of design and digital technology.

We're trying to encourage our people to work in a series of parallel directions and to accept that our findings which, presented to subscribers, are not just the resolution of ideas and projection towards the production of a report. One of the parallels here was to create a certain aesthetic, a certain look that would represent tomorrow. It's not a question of searching for the average, we're not really not interested in raw information. Negotiations of subjectivity have been played out in the most sophisticated way already. We're much more interested to continue a process of suspended resolution, avoiding completion so that we can keep some ideas in the air.

A car is bought, something white and over-powered. Three people get in the vehicle and drive east for three days. They take turns at the wheel. No sleep. At night orange light glows around the dials and switches. Air conditioning sighs and on occasion the side window is cracked open. The noisy bursts of air keep fading drivers awake.

Somebody's going to get their head smashed to oatmeal in a car park.

CONCENTRATION

Our second person is in a bar. Lincoln, talking with people but thinking ahead at all times and coming up with a number of future scenarios while at the same time having a fairly ordinary conversation. Outside a car stalls and a tailback of irritated drivers interrupts the talk. Resumption is immediate once they've got the Toyota out of the way. Three specific examples of taking an idea through a series of developments to a number of micro-conclusions are outlined. Lincoln is working alone now, without giving any data away. No longer speaking to the others who crowd here. Not that it's so many people, just the type who seem to occupy a great deal of space. Three specific examples. Lincoln is struggling to put them together. First thoughts. Keys to the projection model. First attempt. It starts here. Everyday is not the same. That has already been worked out. So it can't be the first idea. In fact there is no premier here, so it is clear that the three scenarios can be read as parallel and mobile. Have a tenth beer. Thank you. And some pretzel sticks filled with a ragged neo-cheese. Thanks again. Smile to the right and back to forward-facing again, looking in the mirror across from a place at the bar. Feeling sick. One. The establishment of a degree of separation between activities, the potential for a competitive presentation of similar things at the same time, all combined with a desire to accept that those things are so samey that it is hardly worth the bother of identifying the differences. Marginalising the activities of the centre. Our reports themselves are not varied, it's just that the way they are presented is different in each case. Good. Detailed changes in attitude towards a mess of things that are no longer essentially the same. Don't let on. Keep people thinking in the short term. Rely upon self-levelling economic chaos. No longer essential at all. Two. The desire to be in a different place tomorrow. Both literally and in terms of what can happen. This is inevitably connected to the sudden appearance of a tendency to move, whether that shifting is desired or willed. Three. Apply this scenario like the other two. Things are coming together now. One and two can be modelled and applied to any number of situations. That will be pedantic. Another beer? Number 25. Yes please. Zoning out. Concentrate. Three, three, three. The possibility of compromise. The way in which desires are proposed pitched against the potential of what can really take place. Fading out for a second there. Out of focus. Thirty pints of beer. Thirty fucking pints of beer. A staggered body found at the bar. Bloated and alone. It's been a long day. It's not possible, about three months, surrounded and frustrated. These three models will be applied. They've been used in the past and they will be again. But later. Now it's time to sleep. Lincoln has something of a drink problem. A narcoleptic first and now a dipsomaniac. The only hope at this stage is for something speedy and someone to help the drying out process. Maybe a third person will fare better at this stage. Things all need naming. Please third person, help us out.

At the same time this third person is making a section-by-section breakdown of an index. Denmark's working hard. Simultaneously the working environment of all three has become increasingly insulated. Ramsgate, Lincoln and Denmark have decided that in order to proceed they must work in increasing isolation. Not just from each other but from everyone else that they might otherwise be forced to come up against. That's what the room stuff was about. No help, no talk, no action. They have now entered a post-communication situation. As a post-script to this section Denmark creates a précis of what he calls the looking-backward syndrome, which is e-mailed to a large number of people. This is crucial, for as the trio look towards the origin of projection, they will need to reclaim past attempts to project into the future, so each must work backwards for a while. Experimenting with twenty-five-hour days was an option for one. It's already been done. No temporal games this time. But, wait a second before being so definitive about what will or will not do. They are being set up. Lincoln is thinking hard, now back in that deep carpet of brown wool. Ramsgate is flying around in a Piper Cub, or a Cherokee Cub or a Bell Huey with a Plexi dome. Or a Pied Apache Piper Cunt. One is working on structure, the second is looking for the place to be. Number three, Denmark. The other one in this tri-tale, is ready with a message. An e-mail message. The second and third person are on the list of recipients, but as yet the text goes unread. Indexing is about to begin and some people are easily distracted.

A knock at three doors. One a house, one an office and the other the cabin door to the flight deck of a plane. In each case there is a gift to be offered. A gun. One large, one middle-sized and one small. It will come in handy. A special way to aid communication. Not direct this time but indirect. A present from the same people. From each to the other. It has some symbolic role all wrapped up in a practicality. A new kind of ceramic that looks like something comforting and familiar. So how new? Doesn't matter. Each is happy and clearly no longer alone. This device will aid their communication with each other. Not yet. Ramsgate is taking a journey. It is autumn and much later on. Go north and the landscape changes. For a trip like this Ramsgate is taking as much stuff as possible. Sports equipment, warm clothing, some ropes and an electronic positioning device. God, business is down in this part of the town. Abandoned but modern. Looking like some people in the past had hope here and then forgot to tell anyone else. Ramsgate likes the way the buildings are optimistic. Parking places, little hierarchical touches. Top offices that could hold some serious meetings. But most are now in a state of disrepair. Locked up and locked out of any dynamic exchange. You couldn't exactly call it industrial decay, but it's close. These were never really industries in terms that can be understood by each of our reporters. They offered services. And some made things. But the raw materiality was unconvincing and badly distributed.

At The Big Conference Centre, so near completion, feigned crisis emerged when a top person enquired about who was responsible for the oversight. An extra room, no a whole floor, had slipped through the net. Yet there would be inner joy for that same top individual as she prepared to perform rapid and expensive corrective surgery on the space. And what a space shone through. Vague beyond question, right up to a realm of visual specificity that had been lazily quashed in all other parts of the conference centre. Those other mass places had been designed with flexibility in mind, of course leaving each with no hope of such vaunted user-friendliness. The problem was all the rest of the building was named as mobile, each space hyper-flexible so reduced to an indication of multiple parameters and possible functions. So only flexibility would work here. Hard to think of anything specific working out. But not with the overlooked place. Not up here. Flexibility was built in almost everywhere else, yet the nature of what became known as 'the discovery crisis' led to a need for a role. And here the top person came with a number of potential solutions and only one real desire. A chance to offer a specific place in a building that was a tribute to vagueness.

Three scenarios arrive by return of post/e-mail:

Tripart
It is night-time in a city. We are not concerned with the details of the streets or any specific building. Instead we sweep across the rooftops. Moving faster than a car and slower than an aeroplane. Reaching the limit of this squared-off place we continue to move across a desert landscape. The view is darkening, yet the sky glows slightly with blue and red. Cut back to the city. A group of people are having a discussion in a bar. We see each face quite clearly. There is a silvered canopy above their heads. Parts of this provisional platform are filled and brightly coloured. The conversation is wide-ranging. Many subjects are covered. How to communicate. How to meet. How to travel. Back out in the desert we are no longer moving. There is a visual stillness combined with a human presence suggested by a heartbeat or a high pitched yet barely audible noise. We move slowly. Then down into the ground. Everything is black.

Back in the city we are now outside the same bar. Three people leave the place where they had been talking. The walls of some of the buildings are clad in aluminium up to a certain height, although this level does vary. Pausing for a moment, the three bid each other good night and head off in different directions. We keep cutting between them as they move on. It starts to rain and we see each of them turn and look up at the sky. They are walking through quite different urban environments by now, all separated by narrow city streets. Above their heads a large corrugated structure is slowly extending from the buildings that line the pavement. Baby blue. Covering and protecting the lone pedestrians from the rain. Time moves faster now. One of the people is a doctor. Every now and then we witness the daily examinations. We learn something of a doctor's life and see a way to operate. Capable of changing the way people look and the way that they feel. The second works with computers. A world mainly confined to an office space half-way up a towering building. Changing the way people understand the world around them and the world within them. The third seems to have no clear job and no obvious social obligations. Abilities best understood as an expression of multiple activities. Something of a mediator and clearly talented. Precise, yet so far having managed to avoid specific allegiance to any set group of activities or responsibilities. Capable of changing the way people think and the way they create and maintain their loyalties.

The question of whether or not these three will meet again is not important. There is some synchronisation of their actions and a certain degree of shared understanding between them. At least it seems that way from our distance. Each of them goes through an adult life, from the age of twenty onwards. We follow their successes and their disasters. The idea of achievement here is relative to their intentions. It is not clear whether the three are good or bad. Their behaviour is rooted in negotiation, compromise and understanding. At all points they seem to experience many things at the same time. We spend an equal amount of time attending to each of them. The neighbourhood effect. Yet this is not exactly obvious because of the way that our understanding of their developing stories is ordered. Although we follow a conventional chronological narrative, it seems to work in three distinct ways. One of the characters is clearly getting older and proceeding towards eventual slowness and potential death. One is getting younger and more enthusiastic while the third seems to remain in a form of the present. It is not the near future or the recent past, but something quite different. Three people, meeting once and never seeing each other again. We are the link between them. And we provide the logic that might be applied to understand their relative status. At some point they will escape the confines of this desiccated place and make their way back towards the city. Maybe the three people are working towards this moment, maybe they are trying to avoid it ever taking place.

Two other scenarios arrive, but the texts are corrupted. Only the titles of attached files make it through. 'Rebate' and 'Proceed' are the names of the other two messages.

We are home now with Denmark. Self created questions. Does it come from our fascination with indexing and the way we analyse potential? Is our think tank connected to the way documentation changes our behaviour? It's a think tank. Narrow and focused.

A car pulls up and a dog jumps out of the open passenger window.

In the end, people will always ask the question, what is the idea behind this report? They prefer projection based on a singularity. We're not influenced by precision, we're reframing it. The project of some earlier strategists was also to try and reframe any question of growth. In their case it was necessary to ask, how can we continue to get richer without completely destroying the planet through revolution or ecological disaster? As a result a lot of think-tank work is about positioning yourself, about remaining inconclusive. It is about the instruction to take a piece of data and put it to your own uses. It has other qualities of course, metaphorical and complex, but it is not a question of playing with precision. We're more interested in negotiating why this centre ground took hold rather than keeping away from it. We look at places where you get compromise, bureaucracy and strategy for political and economic ends. Centre ideas which are much more interesting than the dominant trend of subcultural focus at one extreme and specific analysis at the other. We're dealing with parallel structures, and we like the idea of data and decor in relation to this. But we're not so interested in playing with pure research, whatever that might be. Research and analysis are two problematic areas for us because strategists use them a lot as models for something they have lost, or never had in the first place, namely a large catchment area. We moved away from a fascination with results into the middle, where you get a really dynamic territory which has more to do with how thing are really decided. Projection for us is a hyper analysis, analysis is a hyper experience, it's not something that is useful for any one group. Both are distancing, and our work is distanced enough from the dynamic complex structures already, without it having to go even further away mediated by the world of pure statistics and lumpy analysis.

Denmark feels sick. Purple lumps appearing on grey forearms.

You have to understand that we're only interested in data presentation as it stands as an accusation against us. Some people still have a problem with think tanks. Data we picked up from working with a lot of people shocked us when we realised the implications. Our organisation was prepared to embrace certain issues that were always seen as binary problems. We're looking at the issue of data fragmentation and the question of how a report should look. How do you decode and play with such ideas? Our work has got very little to do with psychology or irony, it's connected with the everyday structural decisions that actually dominate our world.

Two boys enter the north end of a pedestrian subway tunnel.

We're involved in a very simple game about setting up different points of attraction in order to motivate attention. We remain committed to understanding the effects of short attention span but feel that this has always been an issue. We wouldn't expect someone to sit and go through one of our reports. That's the beauty of The Big Conference Centre. People can pick up the ideas they need faster than we can keep them mutating.

We see the boys' progression on closed circuit television. A large group of men are following them.

DIALOGUE

Denmark is in an aeroplane travelling across a developed, well marked landscape. Flying by wire again. Making a series of mental side steps all of which look towards alternative options in relation to the landscape below. Investigating the possibility of expansion rather than mere development. All of the ideas that result are noted on a number of sick bags with a borrowed pen.

We cut between our initial people increasingly quickly. Ramsgate, Lincoln and Denmark. Coca-cola coloured wall sleeper, beige and dark brown furniture in the bar drinker, tartan and silver plane flyer. Each one in turn appearing to reach a point where compromise is the option that offers the most fixed position. At least that's the way it looks at the moment. The necessity to communicate is what leads to this temporary sense of compromise. They all know that they will need new names and they all know that they're going to have to get a lot clearer than this. But that's not the point. Tomorrow, tomorrow, there's always tomorrow, it's only a day away.

Four-hundred guerrillas move into the border region.

Message is as follows:
To whom it may concern. The date of this message is tomorrow. I am looking for two other people. At present I am locked into an indexing phase. Heavy duty. Working on a structure, but with no great quantity of content beyond that which I apply in order to model certain scenarios. I need a location and something more substantial than that quantity of material currently available to myself. The location will require designing. Some thought must go into the look in order to create a series of places within the building which can allow some projection back and forth from material to index and from index to material. A repository for other people's thoughts. Our role is backwards. We offer little more than a degree of development. The potential of the parallel kept in place. What we can do is contrary. The importance of our technique is towards ensuring that no blurring takes place. The focus on indexing enables input to remain pure.

Nothing can become mixed or automatically cross-referenced. While this message has been sent to a vast number of people, it has been made known to me that there are at least two people who could become involved in the use and application of the indexing process that I have been developing. I would hope that those two, wherever they may be, can find the opportunity to reply to this message.

A small boy smiles at his friend.

Give time to absorb the message. Out there on a mission. In the country, near the border.

It's irritating that people talk about the economic system in terms of decay down here. Because no one had really enjoyed working in these places. Now they were all somewhere else, apart from those left behind who looked after the view. So go and stop at a small village, just outside town. Ramsgate has had enough travel for now. Walk through the dark streets. All the stuff brought along for the trip is now safely stashed away. The village is well looked after. Locked up for the night. No one here has a history interwoven with the fabric of the place. All came later in search of something rugged and real. It's Ramsgate remember. The sleeper. He stops his walk back where it had begun. Then into a building occupied by someone well known to this northern traveller. Inside now and then after some food and drink, stories remembered and refined, it is time to sleep. That night something takes place far from the village that will bring all three people closer still. And here in a large bed covered with purple sheets, Ramsgate has a dream. One specific think-tank system, with a new language. An organisation through which to observe the observers. Then something dark and hot overtakes these night thoughts. Vivid and sensual. Caught with increasing images of claustrophobic tension. Warm in the centre and cool enough at the perimeter. There is some stress, legs stiffen. An arm goes numb. Waking then sleeping again. Rubbing hot and cool. A smile and a touch. Slipping now into a non-dream time. Deep sleep at last.
And what does it look like Ron?

Big Conference Centre awaits.

I'm glad that you asked me. Something quite lovely to my eye. Although it's taken some time for me to really lock onto the look. You see it's squared off. Everything shifted to a position where it works at an angle to everything else. Details. It's that squared-off floor in relation to the squared-off ceiling, but both of quite a different scale. The ceiling, you don't notice it at first. Not the most striking area, and this must be partly because of the way they did the floor. All along they had a ceiling planned for this place. The contract for that had been calculated on taking the area of the building and multiplying it by the number of floors in place. This kind of engineered solution was bound to include a forgotten room. The ceiling was the only part of this special place that couldn't be manipulated that was probably for the best. It was due to the fact that the initial impact of the overlooked room was even further heightened when you realised that ceiling was pretty generalised and matched that used in the rest of the place. Makes you wonder sometimes. The ceiling contractors must have known all along.

The characters merge into each other. We have no sense of location. An environment is described that can be altered and contradicted, but we know that it won't be.

It's a fact that the research presentation, digital communication, all finally shown to committee, is very short. Data is missing.

Everything now is the result of a displacement where, in order to think about how to present the findings, we used damaged data as source material with which to construct a series of documentary scenarios. It's not very interesting for us to re-play that whole data-gathering process as some evidence that we did it. It has already been presented elsewhere in the north and west. It was wrong there and it's wrong here.

Ramsgate, Lincoln and Denmark now know that they're sitting on an enormous error.

ASSESSMENT

Of course as the years go by there is more of a chance that the e-mail message will languish unread. There is no hope that Ramsgate and Lincoln will pick it up now. The content is too vague. Nothing is coming together beyond structure. They're not yet sure that they even need any separation devices. Give it time, give it time. Momentary glances are made between one and another across a couple of oceans. Looks inside during times of focus. Origin, search and compilation. The message was ridiculous, what made it necessary? Irrelevant and inadmissible charge. There is no room for ridicule right now. Some work is about to begin and the terms of development are fading into view. If you can't stand in the way of progress then maybe you can hold up a development. Linking brains through isolationist strategies. A lot of time will pass until we discover where things are leading to. Many, many years before we can come back to the three. There will be conclusions eventually and they will be listed with precision. A whole sequence of events noted carefully. Issues addressed and recommendations made. Outside it is starting to rain in three quite different global locations. Fortunately for our report, the three people are all in rainy places tonight. Humming, nodding and winking. A glance to each side and the realisation that they are not really alone, it's just that for now the work must be done in isolation.

A bright morning in three different locations. Ramsgate, flushed and happy. Lincoln dark and nearly broken. Denmark is back in bed, the alarm is about to go off. Let's follow them. Daily business. Get up, eat, wash, walk, work. Each goes about these tasks in a slightly different way. Is there any reason to wonder whose technique is unique to whom? Someone forgot to remind anyone of this. Now each of them are involved in supplying basic foods, materials and services. That journey north wasn't so vague. There is some application of process here. Each of the three will be in a position to better understand the centre once they have all had some serious experience of supply. No competition here. Just a few fundamental set ups all on a small scale. And besides, everyone's got to eat.

Lincoln's happy. Deciding to go public. Put yourself in a more dynamic position to approach Lincoln. Move in rapidly and fast from a long distance. Keep moving low over the rooftops, out to the edge of town. There are thousands of cars parked and some buses rowed neatly up by the river. Rush inside that low-boxed building, over on the far left side of the tightly bordered property. Look it's Lincoln, speaking a language clear to everyone. Speaking like spelling. Everything outlined. How to conciliate. Hosting a seminar around the idea of creating an assessment tank that will permit constant ongoing critique of the way that the near future is presented. Some practical findings are near to discussion, yet this is the old-school presentation style. It is a fine summer morning. It may well be, but. It's not going to be enough. At present Lincoln's style is just reportage. Yet people are happy. They are an audience and they want to be efficient at it. Denmark on the other hand is sitting in a small summer house, still working on that section-by-section breakdown. Heavy duty indexing going on and on. That's what the out of town audience is missing. One member of that attentive group is finding it hard to concentrate. Get up and make your way towards a side exit. Smoothing down the back of a jacket and holding a dignified look forwards. Walking steadily now and with some purpose. Pressing on the door handle. Deep breath and some surprise that the door leads immediately to the outside.

We see the beauty of the countryside as it's experienced by this ex-listener. Why not follow as he takes a trip through the local countryside? Hey, a group of small children. Maybe twenty of them. Unreasonably quiet and all close enough to speak to. Let's go together. The former audience member and a group of strange children. Walking with a firm stride and crossing out of any developed area. Across a field that forms the last impression of development here. Now into an open area dotted with occasional trees. There are people here who come every year or two, but it's hard to find those places where they hang out. There must be one focal point here somewhere. Yes there to the left, past that clump of low scrub oak. A staging post and viewing place. Sit underneath and argue. Just you and the kids. Denmark is in mid-flow.

An increasing realisation that the issue of concentration is not merely restricted to this idea of exchange but can depend on focus. Things might not be as bad as they first seem. What kind of country is this anyway? Concentrate hard upon the possible development of those children will you, our friendly ex-audience member.

Ramsgate, Lincoln and Denmark come and go all the time now. It's hard to keep up. They are gathering together a mass of stuff and now moving closer all the time. Triplicate. Each going through an elaborate series of arrivals and departures in many different situations, but never crossing paths. At least five years pass and all we see are comings and goings. Nothing more gets done.

The same old ceiling contract that was viewed as sufficient for the rest of the conference centre will be applied to the overlooked place. It sends a frisson of pleasure when you realise that this better space has the same old topping. Suspended. What a floor-ceiling combination.

We sense the three people at work at every moment, yet their presence is only in the background for a while, and we see the way certain urban structures have developed. Our out-of-focus view of them pulls into a clear image. We notice only the differences that have been wrought over the five-year period. The first person is playing a game. The second person is creating a series of complex tasks for a number of other people, while the third person establishes a complex database that works to anticipate and thereby accentuate progression and change for individual benefit. Think-tank systems are used to monitor these events so each person has to compromise and instead set up a parallel way of working and explaining instead of having the illusion of ploughing onwards.

A child reflects upon what has taken place. We suddenly race through this child's entire life right through to the moment near their possible loss of interest and stimulation, in what they experience around them. At the point where it is nearly too late, all three people appear together for the first time and attempt to prevent this exit from ideas. They try to do this by playing with time to such an extent that the moment is not reversed, it is merely suspended. Postponed indefinitely.

Ramsgate's speaking.

The fundamental changes that led to our sense of development are connected to the use of projection and scenarios. What happens to you when you realise that every day is not the same? Before that, when people generally believed in God or in a given system of social structures, every day was kind of the same. Once this idea was challenged you got the possibility of sophisticated economic projection. When you get a domination of projection you also get the possibility of capitalism, because you can decide, well, maybe next week I would like to be in this position, I'm currently selling ten pairs of socks a week but I would like to project that in a week's time I'll be selling twenty pairs of socks. Of course, if you believe in older religious structures, your place was to sell ten pairs of socks, it was not to sell twenty pairs of socks a week because God had given you your place, and your place was to sell ten pairs of socks and tough shit if you starved. Of course people contradicted this model, but it held up pretty well until the Industrial Revolution. So this question of projection is central, linked to an attempt to become as flexible as the most dynamic systems in the society. While strategists try to become more and more authentic, and more analytical, they also get on with deciding what it's going to be like tomorrow. We still use the idea of projection on a day-to-day basis as the replacement for far-reaching utopias. So we investigate the idea of projection in order to claim and keep it from being used by dynamic groupings. We now have an obligation to spend most of our time looking at the history and genealogy of the idea of projection and tomorrowism.

Said Ramsgate.

Our work always involves a period of history where fundamental changes happen in the behaviour of people who were previously locked into precisely maintained social strata.

Yes Denmark.

We're not very interested in the central conceptions of future trends. We have nothing to do with discovering the potential of tomorrow or engaging in socio-political pre-archaeology. If central concepts are central concepts, it is often due to compromise, and an ability to communicate. Therefore we're interested in people who are not very good at communicating. And that's where secondary analysts come in, because they are often the ones who have the interesting ideas, which are difficult to get across effectively. Such analysts are sometimes secondary due to the communication effect. We like think-tank models that are very good at communicating but we're not interested to make another one. We're curious as to where this modern sense of effective communication comes from and therefore how to take it further, we're not trying to be cute by looking at these secondary organisations in isolation. It's just interesting for us to deal with concepts beyond communication. Confused and ambiguous, but essential.

In think-tank scenarios, projection is very quickly linked with conspiracy. That's why we're interested in modelling an analysis of analysis. But we're not so deluded to think all the meaning and the ideas in our research exist in that one particular location. The Big Conference Centre is not the ultimate location for all our strategy, so why should we think that the meaning of our research resides in a single report? The location for analysis doesn't necessarily have to be the site of data itself anymore. We have a problem with the idea of 'a' client, singular, we don't believe in it at all and we are often shocked by the retarded conception of clients that exists within the world of statistical analysis. We always try to acknowledge the non-client, we're not interested in group mentality. If you come to The Big Conference Centre you cannot go away with any shared ideas, in fact, you should keep in mind that the most dynamic effects are often created by the mirage of analysis which disguises a writhing mass of contradictions and ongoing attempts to redefine projected relationships.

A body twitches, pressed into the roof of a Toyota. A fireman tells a joke. Through the pain the body smiles. Tries to laugh at the absurdity of being broken on a hardtop. Lincoln, Denmark and Ramsgate move up to the shattered window. Down below in the crowd a young man points up at them as they peer down, fresh wind on their faces.

LITERALLY NO PLACE
A group of people return to a commune, to check some things. This text looks at the proliferation of communal environments, from the campus model of software companies to the free structures of the Diggers in San Francisco. Using a re-examination of BF Skinner's WALDEN 2 as a starting point, the book describes various attempts to understand new models of communality in light of new recognitions of difference. The text is interspersed with autobiographical sections that introduce various themes, such as the notion of the post-industrial, the effect of peers and siblings on behaviour and the desire to return to more profound social relationships. The ideas in this book lead towards the work surrounding the infinitely suspended book CONSTRUCCION DE UNO which proceeded to look at the implications of group work and post-Fordist production models in more detail.

LITERALLY NO PLACE
COMMUNES, BARS AND GREENROOMS
Ethics, Conscience and the Revision of Form
in the Built World

PART 1

CHILDREN OF NINE OR TEN ARE DRAGGED FROM THEIR
SQUALID BEDS AT TWO, THREE OR FOUR O'CLOCK IN THE
MORNING, AND COMPELLED TO WORK FOR A BARE
SUBSISTENCE UNTIL TEN, ELEVEN OR TWELVE AT NIGHT,
THEIR LIMBS WEARING AWAY, THEIR FRAMES DWINDLING,
THEIR FACES WHITENING, AND THEIR HUMANITY ABSOLUTELY
SINKING INTO A STONE-LIKE TORPOR, UTTERLY HORRIBLE TO
CONTEMPLATE.[1]

They turned in the ravine and climbed to the top of a bank,
just to see the place again. Gone for three days, they had
walked about one hundred kilometres. It felt like half that
distance and could have been double. Some of the group
had been reluctant to leave at first and even more disturbed
to realise that they had walked a semi-looping trail. There
had been no general purpose over the last few days, just
walking for the sake of getting out of the place for a while.
Lacking in focus but productive in the way it blocked their
working process and turned them in on themselves. There
was a strong desire to return rather than press on and
beyond. Never speaking, never planning together, they had
allowed themselves to swing in an arc. Walking had been
the only option anyway. The last car had left some time ago
and the only remaining truck had a transmission completely
drained of fluid that whined and screeched, even when they
tried to improvise some lubrication with home-improved
hydraulic fluid. So they had set off on foot. On hot feet held
by frayed footwear and towards the end, no shoes at all.

The stiffness and soreness that had struck them from the
second day had soon been walked off and their legs had
grown strong. Their step was light and they could feel the
ball of each foot pushing the earth down from them as they

walked. Walking at speed, mainly at night, hadn't been so bad. Short bursts, no consistent pace. Keeping shady, keeping loose. They knew they had no heading and they had paced themselves to make sure they would be able to complete the curving, parallel trip, without ever feeling that they were circling back. Arcing around, keeping the sun to the left. For some there were blisters and fluid filled socks and limping and the use of sticks, but they were a fit group. Strong enough to bear a journey like this.

It was noon. A group of people turning past an outcrop and seeing the commune again. People in a desert place, who had been trying to escape from being shown everything, coming back to have a look once more, coming back to check everything. To see the semi-autonomous, survivalist place that had to be tested, checked and played with —requiring a ship-like departure and return, to see the clumped low buildings fading then coming close once more. Needing to know what the place looked like from a distance and always holding close the idea that there might be no return. There had been moments when they had strayed off the parallel path yet had always cut back to ensure eventual return to the commune. An environment that lacked a particular sentimentality. A particular memory. Loaded with the debris of their earlier work. And now refreshed as a new place. A flashed reminder of what it had been at the outset.

We are in a situation that is somehow reduced and is certainly distracted. They have returned to try and recreate something, jump-start their procedures, get going once more with some projection of a rinsed place or new location. To catch the idea of a commune, a functional rationalist commune that can really work and be productive. Trying to function without falling into certain traps. Retaining a semi-autonomous relationship to the outside world in order to make a point about what might be possible. For all the time that they had been involved, something had been missed and a degree of play had been avoided. At all times testing and checking had been the root of their involvement, but now they also wanted to catch the moments that had been glossed over. And after a few days outside they had picked up a new form of dry exchange. Games and play taking form as distracted yet sharpened discourse. Now they wanted to go back and return some favours. Lock themselves down with less talk and less listening. Go in through the gates again but this time to offer some models for exchange that slide beyond the dynamic contentment of the compound. Tie up and root around in some systems that had been subjugated by their eagerness to merely prove their parallel system could work. Function was not the long-term problem. The production of ideas was flagging and weakening under the weight of self-justification. They were not ready to be sub-cultural, but something more complicated, more relaxing, more diffident.

So maybe their mission could be expressed as a beach-towel. They could take a phrase and use it. Maybe "My step was light and I could feel the ball of each foot pushing the earth down from me as I walked". Relocate the words and read them at a glance while walking by on the beach, (the desert will have to suffice for now, they haven't seen the sea for some time). It's maybe the only line of a real thinking produced by this commune. It's the only moment of functional poetry. A pause and description of stoppage before non-action. A moment when shifted attitudes take on fresh structure; it's the flickering, stalling, micro-conclusion where our group somehow expresses some real belief in the world of the commune and dodge round the formation of a compound. They specialise in arresting their own procedures before seeing them activated. This commune is a place where the design of the trays is better than in the outside world. Where people are free because they cannot really communicate, where they are free because they are stuck. This is a place where they produce new forms of classically derived music, keeping things locked in a region of quality and disengagement. Distraction and play in this place are always unnecessarily complicated. Setting themselves in one year and flashing back to another. Creating love stories. Going to sleep one day and waking up again at another time. Making things out of other things. Taking each other apart and putting each other together again. Picturing a perfect projection of a communal afternoon. Sitting by the window, looking out as people move objects from one place to another. Some revision and relocation of utopian communities is bound to take place, but has now been transferred into a self-consciously 'just before' and 'just after' time, with all the attendant implications of that continual transfer.

Our group of people had joined together, left and then returned in order to revisit this renewed community and they are absolutely post-war people. Any war, declared or not. They are from the moment when people were involved in action before the learning process had a chance to take root. They are people who have come back. People who have had an interrupted education. They are people who have been deeply involved, for one reason or another, and we are catching them before they have had time to reflect but during moments of continual reconstruction. For that reason the seriousness of their future actions will shatter once they return to the commune. This is a group of people who can easily be transferred in time, continually spinning off and rejoining towards the rebuilding of a functional relationship. They have a soft research necessity. A need to come and somehow project a place where they can be both controlled and free. Where their sense of ethics and conscience can be collectivised, where they can be both pulled together and gently teased apart. They want to be communal without being communistic—a very precise distinction. They want to know the nature of their community without employing an essentialist logic as a carrier of their complexity.

View it all from a distance. The group has a proximity to the recent events of war and a simultaneous distance from all war. Pulled and stretched away from the location of action. Victims of a reprocessing procedure that is immediate, reflective and deliberate. Pulling back a hand from a flame and putting it back still closer this time. Their choice of desert location requires a survivalist mentality without a definable threat. They will always have to look out for stupid accidents. Self-produced micro-crises. Irony states. The potential of post-conflict reconfiguration, both literal and social. These things are important for them but create heightened proto-hierarchical structures. The immediate future departs from the quasi-communist potential of their intentions. Their place could be read as a prevision of subsequent moves in the development of capitalism in the twentieth century and the confused moral and ethical implications of those revised working practices at the beginning of the twenty-first. Compound mentality masquerading as a communal remodelling of working environments. The illusion of security and free exchange, overwritten by rhetoric and corrupted language. What they are really thinking about is a model for living, a model for the appropriation of a certain form of language; they are talking on a daily basis about the establishment of a communal system without any sentimentality for communism. A desire to retain a certain lifestyle and a certain creativity without the attendant problems of control or prediction or planning. Speculative situations running over and swamping daily activity. Speculation as a collective way of action.

In their commune they played with projection. Announcing itself as a non-planned sequence of ideas. As something that can only happen as a result of collective desire and pleasure rather than as a result of a clearly framed set of functional, ethical, markers. This connection between the idea of a communal place that is based on desire and a rupture from a communistic system has a soft connection to their contemporary environment. It is a loose connection that permits exposure of shifts in strategy towards appropriation of better conscience-based and ethically driven ideas. Not counter-cultures but the appropriation of an ethical language within a collective and fractured sense of progress. All tied to a localist neo-conservative nostalgia.

A perfect paradoxical shift of meaning and intention. When our communal revisitors think for a moment about the potential appropriation of counter cultures, they are in a better position to articulate the possession of certain behaviours and structures, as defined by their ability to encompass and reflect an ethical lapse. They are shadowed and shadows; they have a phantom conscience in circulation around them by virtue of their presence in a construction and by their participation in a continual restructuring. For our small group of visitors, living in the commune initially appeared to be a description of rationalist heaven, a perfect place, an organised place, a place that could be better and was constantly accelerating towards an even more precise vision of how things might be. The ends wrenched free from the means towards continual respeculation instead of planning for a perfect, harmonious present. They live the conditions described by their desires. Their entire living and working time may be read as a functional pre-vision of extreme post-management meandering. Soft analysis burning slowly. A move from what you could describe as the excess of context surrounding decision making, towards an attempt to predict in a situation where prediction has come loose from the idea of planning. Where projection has ensured that they have to deal with shorter and shorter time frames. A completely revised sense of the relationship between the individual, the place and the nature of production. Towards discussion of potential action and suppression of activated modes of exchange. The function and use of creative thought as a fetish, rather than a paradigm shift in behaviour or action.

PART 2

THE UTOPIAN IMPULSE IN THINKING IS ALL THE STRONGER,
THE LESS IT OBJECTIFIES ITSELF AS UTOPIA—A FURTHER
FORM OF REGRESSION—WHEREBY IT SABOTAGES ITS OWN
REALISATION. OPEN THINKING POINTS BEYOND ITSELF. FOR ITS
PART, SUCH THINKING TAKES A POSITION AS A FIGURATION OF
PRAXIS WHICH IS MORE CLOSELY RELATED TO A PRAXIS TRULY
INVOLVED IN CHANGE THAN IN A POSITION OF MERE OBEDIENCE
FOR THE SAKE OF PRAXIS. BEYOND ALL SPECIALISED AND
PARTICULAR CONTENT, THINKING IS ACTUALLY AND ABOVE ALL
THE FORCE OF RESISTANCE, ALIENATED FROM RESISTANCE
ONLY WITH GREAT EFFORT.[2]

Sitting now on a ridge, overlooking the commune. It is time
to review three circling tales. The revisitors have some things
to share. And their three stories are located in very specific
environments. They have self-set a tricked-up time game.
An opportunity to express new forms of ongoing ethics and
conscience-based reassessments within a post-planned
world. They have to contribute something. Bring some
stories. Encouraged to reflect, they have to go beyond the
conjuring of some non-places. Look for some moments.
Keep progressing without locking into an oppositional frame.
The listeners know something, but they understand very
little. As they sit a sheet is passed round. A brief outlining of
the way things might go. A reflection upon the first thoughts
of those who turned back.

The first presentation will involve a person and a reflection of
that person. A story set in a small village to the west of an
island country. The second will take place in a bar.
Somewhere on the border, until now shielded from within
and beyond. The last will encompass all three. Sitting in a
greenroom. Waiting to present. Bringing everything together.
Fractured thoughts combined in a mess of pre-reflection
and post-anticipation.

PART 3

THE DISTINCTION BETWEEN PLACES AND NON-PLACES DERIVES FROM THE OPPOSITION BETWEEN PLACE AND SPACE. AN ESSENTIAL PRELIMINARY HERE IS THE ANALYSIS OF THE NOTIONS OF PLACE AND SPACE SUGGESTED BY MICHEL DE CERTEAU. HE HIMSELF DOES NOT OPPOSE 'PLACE' AND 'SPACE' IN THE WAY THAT 'PLACE' IS OPPOSED TO 'NON-PLACE'. SPACE FOR HIM, IS A 'FREQUENTED PLACE', 'AN INTERSECTION OF MOVING BODIES': IT IS THE PEDESTRIANS WHO TRANSFORM A STREET (GEOMETRICALLY DEFINED AS A PLACE BY TOWN PLANNERS) INTO A SPACE.[3]

The first revisitor is already speaking.
"… one of those small villages close to the sea. A place that receives the best and the worst of the prevailing weather. Our focus is clearly on one of two young boys. And this central figure has a shadow, a mirror, and this reflection is his cousin. There are some secondary tales to tell. One involves a Neolithic mound sitting close to a low house. The environment is constantly overwritten by a sub-story involving a Neolithic burial mound, a number of children and a stolen dagger. Throughout this time you have the effect and influence of two locations, one urban and one non-urban. The relationship is only transitory, taking place every now and then. You have a person and his cousin. You have an idea of two people who are brought up apart but under the same cultural conditions. Their backgrounds are shaped together and apart. They experience the same things in different locations. A story of development and compliance. Good behaviour and bad behaviour and the perception of those things within two very separate environments. Both of these places stimulate sets of equivalent action that are expressed with nuanced differences. A small Neolithic burial mound surrounded by a set of low houses. Someone designed modern houses around an ancient monument. Celebrated death wrapped by mediated life, punctured by juvenile exchange.

"And it is the height of summer. Part of a long day with a temperature like cold spring. And on this day you have a number of small children lolling around on the grass surrounded by a boy and his cousin. All the children and the boy and his cousin are the same age. And the cousin has a stolen dagger. He has no intention of using it. He has every intention of sharing it. Yet the situation is not clear. Part of an exchange of power and knives that emerges in connection to the idea of what happens when neighbourhood relations get complicated—when there is an encouragement to go a sufficient distance away and be disruptive. Not directly instructed, but made completely effective through chaotic abuse of both sides of a fence. The use of children as a controlled chaotic tool. A revelling in anarchic behaviours that can happily be punished by both sides but only resented by one. The use of children as a way to exacerbate problems.

"This space is rendered active by the idea of a small community surrounding a Neolithic mound with a number of children wandering daily and one of them has a stolen dagger, or rope, or some piping or just chapped fists. You have to deal with the idea of how these children are used in order to determine social relationships among small houses around a Neolithic burial mound in a village not far from the sea. Although the idea of a dagger could be resolved in a completely fixed and punishable set of moral conditions, the presence of this knife is essential to the dynamic of all relationships here. Children being used to emphasise and exaggerate ethical conditions in a small community surrounding a Neolithic burial mound (sitting in the middle) and representing an extreme history of place and a paganistic connection to country community. A village of modern bungalows. A boy coming from an urban environment into another environment. Into familiar architecture surrounded by something uncertain. Into familiar stories and intuitive analysis. Familiar forms of entertainment and television loading behaviour. A heightened sense of punishment, behaviour, localism and individuality. Where logic is shared and the imperative to act is not held in check by the dynamic of context. "Stories are shared in this place. All in order to maintain a non-urban sense of spiralling ethics. A man is driving in his car while telling the story of another man who had driven in a different car along the same stretch of road close to small mines, not far from the sea. And that other car had gone into the quicksand. The quicksand formed parts of a tidal river estuary. You have to come back there night after night in the dark; you have to escape from the bungalows around the Neolithic burial mound. And go to look at the tidal river estuary and the quicksand, peer long and hard to see the finger of the man who had been driving too close to the bank. Who had driven into the softening dusk. Settled and glued, sucked down into the semi-solid, half-liquid. And this viewing might be part of some corrective process that is ill defined but needs to be stated. Using children in order to create and play with their role as heightened messengers. It might still be possible to see the finger of that man poking out of the sand but you would have to look very carefully and if you looked that hard, you might see it as much as you might see anything else on a dark night. Close to the sea. A trickle of tidal water cutting through micro-canyons of soft sand leaking down towards the south-west.

"Some mining took place in this area and the mining happened at a moment before the idea of mining as an organised activity had been established and defined—when mining was more like digging a hole and taking things out as fast as possible overlaid with shadows, magic and flickers between—I deserve this—I deserve this not. The mining took place in particular locations, but most have been actively forgotten. You might encounter a bay or an area of water and find out that mining had won, going from the land out under the sea. All achieved without developed forms of industrial technology. Not so different from the way it continues now but shifted enough in terms of attitude and fear. There remains an original doubt about the possibility of a simple action being feasible without complex means. This all ensures that the area is peppered with former mines even if there is no surface trace of the former activity. Some erased, some forgotten, some denied. So the urban child and his cousin, the country child, whenever they are involved in any act that might still be described as a homogenising or amplification of the disputes and the unspoken arguments between the people in the bungalows placed around the

Neolithic burial mound, have the potential to fall down mine shafts. Every moment spent in this location is somehow affected by the potential of falling down holes on the way to do things that are wrongish and rightish simultaneously.

"Of course, there are punctuated everydays too. The country cousin climbs the rocks by the sea and cannot get down again. The helicopters have to come and get him back from the clifftop. There is a desire to climb up things while the other watches. The urban child kept in check while the country child demonstrates the country sensibility. The country sensibility involves the desire to climb a rock without caring if you can get down again. Enjoying the idea that people might think that he can't get down and they might well be right. And, for sure, the helicopter people are quite happy to take their machines out and ride them over to the place where the rock is jagged: taking part in a demonstration of not being quite sure but knowing that they are involved in action. Thumping and hovering and then tipping forwards before jogging to the side and away.

"Later, walking proudly out of the sea and being hit from behind by a particularly big wave and then getting dragged out along the bottom of the sea across the sharp sand and stones. Held by green water and dragged out while everyone is looking down or around. Dragged out quite far. Feeling one hundred metres of undertow. Then surfacing in the water and knowing the warmth of blood running. A soon to be scarred chest scoured along a graded base. Sanded skin. A sense of intuitive struggle. A desire to create complex relationships around the things that are constantly being done on behalf of the people who live in the bungalows beside the Neolithic tomb. People who are happy to watch children testing and probing other children with stolen daggers.

"The discovery of a metal go-kart which no one can remember having bought. And can't remember when or where it was built. And it's too heavy to use and it looks like something more made than bought. It looks like something that could be perfect. It's a bit like that trip to the house where the man had been building a hovercraft. All bound up with the idea of moving away, of escaping the compression of the city and creating something that is part of a fragmented communal environment, without the inconvenience of other people and all that hanging around. The creation of a really useful multi-transport system that only works running around fields in a village placed close to a tomb. A continual prototype. Locked in constant development.

"The country cousin falls out of a tree and onto a road. He is not killed but his arm is fractured and compressed. Part of the bone of his forearm begins to grow as a lump alongside his wrist. Some time later the cousin's father falls out of a building. He falls out of a loading bay punched into the side of a granite structure but doesn't get hurt beyond some bruising. People are getting high, shambolic and deeply disturbed. The evidence of these expanding moments and their effects are not clear, just shifting—continually re-worked and wiped clean each morning. The cousin's bones are developing in strange directions. One darkening afternoon he decides to run to the nearest town but falls. A stick gets stuck in his knee. Slipping at the first turn. Three people standing in the woods. They don't know what to do. They were trying to make a fire, and now they are trying to see through the gloom.

"Run to the nearest town. The cousin turned and said, 'OK, I am going to run to the nearest town'. The other two could not be bothered to listen to this anymore. The nearest town was so far away that you couldn't possibly run to it. So he decided to run and fell, getting a stick stuck in his knee, slipping at the first turn. Carry him home. Carry him back to the house where people are sitting and watching. And the stick is removed from his knee. It is pulled out of his knee slowly but with accelerating crackles of agonising pain.

"Two days later, the cousin and his cousin sit in an old stable block while older people shoot guns over their heads. You can see these two sitting in a stable building. Dividing walls only go half-way up to form places where the horses used to stand. The older people are leaning on the furthest divider and shooting guns towards the other end of the stable. Half-way down this new-use structure two children sit down on the ground. Absorbing the velocity as bullets zip overhead. Listening to a demonstration of original sentimentality. With a rodent shuffle the cousin stands up. Grinning as bullets lick by. He is down again before anyone can hold fire. Tempers have been shattered. The shooters approach. Swiftly removed from his place, he is taken outside and badly beaten by the gun toters. This is a country environment. A Neolithic country environment is just a normal place around the corner where children are used to exaggerate and amplify the codes of a particular place. The gun players are terrified that they might have shot a gurning kid. The beating is severe but ineffectual. It won't work. They are scared that they might have really injured him. His timing had been fractionally charged. So they damage him slowly to make some point. About knowing but never sharing the non-event."

PART 4

MOREOVER, IT SEEMS THAT THE ANY-SPACE-WHATEVER TAKES
ON A NEW NATURE HERE. IT IS NO LONGER, AS BEFORE,
A SPACE THAT IS DEFINED BY PARTS WHOSE LINKING UP
AND ORIENTATION ARE NOT DETERMINED IN ADVANCE, AND
CAN BE DONE IN AN INFINITE NUMBER OF WAYS. IT IS NOW
AN AMORPHOUS SET WHICH HAS ELIMINATED THAT WHICH
HAPPENED AND ACTED IN IT. IT IS AN EXTINCTION OR A
DISAPPEARING, BUT ONE WHICH IS NOT OPPOSED TO THE
GENETIC ELEMENT. IT IS CLEAR THAT THE TWO ASPECTS ARE
COMPLEMENTARY, AND RECIPROCALLY PRESUPPOSE EACH
OTHER: THE AMORPHOUS SET IN FACT IS A COLLECTION OF
LOCATIONS OR POSITIONS, WHICH COEXIST INDEPENDENTLY
OF THE TEMPORAL ORDER, WHICH MOVES FROM ONE PART
TO THE OTHER, INDEPENDENTLY OF THE CONNECTIONS
AND ORIENTATIONS WHICH THE VANISHED CHARACTERS
AND SITUATIONS GAVE TO THEM. THERE ARE THEREFORE
TWO STATES OF THE ANY-SPACE-WHATEVER, OR TWO KINDS
OF 'QUALISIGNS'; QUALISIGNS OF DECONNECTION AND OF
EMPTINESS. THESE TWO STATES ARE ALWAYS IMPLIED IN EACH
OTHER, AND WE CAN ONLY SAY THAT THE ONE IS 'BEFORE' AND
THE OTHER 'AFTER'. THE ANY-SPACE-WHATEVER RETAINS ONE
AND THE SAME NATURE; IT NO LONGER HAS CO-ORDINATES,
IT IS A PURE POTENTIAL, IT SHOWS ONLY PURE POWERS AND
QUALITIES, INDEPENDENTLY OF THE STATES OF THINGS OR
MILIEUX WHICH ACTUALISE THEM.[4]

Waiting and now speaking, the second revisitor has a story
to tell. "Enough flipping of cause and repression. Much later.
A car sits at the edge of the largest parking zone. A corner
of reclaimed land that borders the airport. There are a
number of parking lots, each one precisely named. Driven
through the large country, the cars now sit right at the edge
of the largest parking lot, hard against the reclaimed land
that borders the airport. A developed moment of private
thinking. The use of 'Pink Elephant' instead of 'Parking
Systems Inc'. This last spot bears the most diversified,
faded potential of the place, 'Red Rooster Parking' formerly
known as 'International Car Parks Limited'. Here designation
shifts on a regular basis. Parking used to be centralised, car

parking used to be owned by the airport. We are on reclaimed land better named as recycled. Waiting to rotate again into new airport expansion. Ownership of the car park changes hands without comment or notice. Constantly reclaiming and renaming the land by the airport. Process upon process and the shaving of function.

"They pick up a car and then they go. Night-time arrival in a small town coated in snow. Which leads to the idea that the small town is often coated in snow but in fact this is a one-off thing. Tempered coating affects understanding of the place. It should take eighteen hours to drive from one end of the country to the other. So there are the moments on the highway when the passenger falls asleep. During this time the car encounters fog and the driver is passed with a hum swoosh by another, driving at speed. Glancing at the passenger and noticing even breathing and calm closed eyes, the driver pulls out behind the speeding passer for a short high. Just to capture the sensation of moving fast through zero visibility. Driving through fog. Getting ultra-sensible. A sense of someone sleeping. And a sense of another car driving past with its red light dodging into the distance. Glancing at the person still sleeping. Pull out. And if the speeding passer has to stop we will join them, compacted and stunned blue into the parcel shelf, the passenger seat and the road beyond. Moving fast through zero visibility. Low planes flying through grounded cloud. (Pilots seem happier during intermittent cloud. It is a rare moment of relative passage.) The sleeping passenger wakes. But the car is slowing down once more and the fog has given way to clear. On a short coffee stop, the two passengers hear the sound of people shooting, so don't speak. Small migrating birds are getting hit and missed.

"Towards the border there are two additional people in the car. They must have been picked up somewhere along the way. There is an argument between these two newcomers and the passenger in the car. One of the new people attempts to run away from the vehicle while it's going through a customs checkpoint. Fragmented, they had met volunteer firemen in country bars who had told them where to find standing stones. Forest fires clear the brush. On the way back from meeting the firemen, the driver briefly misreads a curve in the road and gently bumps onto the verge, not checking speed, only direction. One of the passengers feigns sleep having heard that total relaxation mitigates the effect of accidents.

"And everything leads to a bar, because we are now in that bar. Very early in the morning before light cracks through. A precise description of paranoid hangover. Liquid removed between the synapses of the brain so a faster connection of mental activity can take place for a while before overload sets in. A heightened sense of being in a bar early in the morning about five minutes before dawn. There is nothing to listen to in this bar. And the only question is whether Audrey Hepburn is English or American. Someone says she is Japanese. Which is not unreasonable under the circumstances—and funnyish.

"Someone has put together a book with photographs of every drink available in this bar, good breakfast reading material. And they haven't cheated even though they could have used the same photo for gin and tonic and vodka and tonic. There are short versions of favourite songs on the jukebox but it's too early to listen to them all over again. Super short with the pleasure of each one fading out too quickly following the initial excitement of well-known introductions once more. Dropping away. A mechanism full of familiar tracks, racked up with favourite songs by familiar people. All the songs now last between a minute or two and you would never want to bet on pleasure lasting beyond that opening shot. There is only a continual and repeated desire for the bulk of a song to get underway but it fades before settling down into repetitive strain. Jukeboxing and completely shut down.

"Some bikers come into the bar to eat rabbit and tripe. Happy to be closing on the border. Leather boys eating pets. One person leaves and takes a piss over the wall while looking out towards the sea. The sea is 200 miles away. Someone arrives with a record and puts it in the jukebox.

The bar users are supposed to wait for a jukebox company representative. Jimmy the jukebox opener. The label on the legend will not be changed until the man comes from head office to change it. Until then the new song will have to sit under another title. The local is always dissipated and heightened next to the border. But now these bar people have found the soundtrack to another longing. A set of lyrics and a crypto-logic. They are in the bar in the morning with something new to listen to. In a bar close to the border. Every other record on the jukebox is in the local language. But this new one speaks American. Someone has arrived and levered open the jukebox. But they can't change the label. The label remains the same. Only the local people in the bar know where to find the song. They can share this perfect conspiracy. This terrible record. Found under another title for now and for a while to come. It makes them happy. Describing a narcissistic non-place lathered in coke.

"Lying on top of a building, the clouds looked no nearer than they had when I was lying on the street. Everybody would consider this to be a complete disaster. The local area produces light-bulbs, special light-bulbs for films. Bulbs to be used as lamps for particular situations. And all the workers drink a lot because the place where they are working is basically the only place that's working; it's the only place that appears to be functioning like a factory. Everyone else in the area might as well be building their own vision of a hovercraft. Building personal hovercrafts and boats for themselves out of concrete. People tend to fall out of the factory rather than face the reality of being the only neo-collective concern. They are all functioning on the cusp of accidents and rarely wait for them to happen."

PART 5

IN THE REALM OF TERRITORIAL DEVELOPMENT, 'TIME' NOW
COUNTS MORE THAN 'SPACE'. BUT IT IS NO LONGER A MATTER
OF SOME CHRONOLOGICAL 'LOCAL TIME', AS IT ONCE WAS,
BUT OF UNIVERSAL 'WORLD TIME', OPPOSED NOT ONLY TO THE
LOCAL SPACE OF A REGION'S ORGANISATION OF LAND, BUT TO
THE WORLD SPACE OF A PLANET ON THE WAY TO BECOMING
HOMOGENEOUS.

FROM THE URBANISATION OF THE REAL SPACE OF NATIONAL
GEOGRAPHY TO THE URBANISATION OF THE REAL TIME OF
INTERNATIONAL TELECOMMUNICATIONS, THE 'WORLD SPACE'
OF GEOPOLITICS IS GRADUALLY YIELDING ITS STRATEGIC
PRIMACY TO THE 'WORLD TIME' OF A CHRONOSTRATEGIC
PROXIMITY WITHOUT ANY DELAY AND WITHOUT ANY
ANTIPODES.[5]

So what they have to think about are time-based excursions
into the management of time. Letting days slip by as they
attempt to work out how to become more efficient. Exchange
and control are under reconsideration. Exchange of ideas
and production intertwined and excessively analysed. Think
about application of technology to the organisation of time.
Formulating new programmes that can operate within and
around the potential of the place. The lamp factory lamps
are used in the making of films. The only factory, the only
place in this bar-ridden environment where there is the
memory and projection of an idea of productive work. Where
there might be some echoes of earlier visions of how to get
better. This factory is the first factory that has ever been
seen in these parts, yet it's a factory that produces unique
things. It never produces the same thing twice, it makes
lamps to order, it makes special lamps. It is the first and last
working place in an environment laden with the illusion of
personal progress. Set up against the potential of the
commune it is a collapsed place. But instead of coming up
with a holistic method of survival it has developed a multi-
vision that is locked down and super limited.

PART 6
ALTHOUGH WE ARE USED TO THE IDEA OF A SOCIETY
IN WHICH ECONOMIC RELATIONS ARE ANARCHIC
(THE ESSENCE OF A MARKET-BASED ECONOMY), THE IDEA OF
POLITICAL ANARCHY IS CHALLENGING. YET GLOBAL SOCIETY
IS A SOCIETY IN WHICH ANARCHY PREVAILS AT BOTH THESE
CRUCIAL LEVELS OF SOCIAL ORGANISATION. THE ECONOMIC
SYSTEM OF GLOBAL SOCIETY IS AT ROOT THAT OF THE GLOBAL
MARKET, COORDINATING AN ENORMOUSLY COMPLEX DIVISION
OF LABOUR IN THE PRODUCTION AND EXCHANGE OF
COMMODITIES. THE POLITICAL SYSTEM OF GLOBAL SOCIETY IS
BASICALLY THAT OF THE COMPETITIVE INTERNATIONAL SYSTEM
OF STATES, COORDINATING AN EQUALLY COMPLEX DIVERSITY
OF NATIONAL-STATE POLITICS. THE GLOBAL CULTURAL SYSTEM
IS LARGELY ONE OF DIVERSE, PART-INTEGRATED NATIONAL AND
SUB-NATIONAL CULTURES ORGANISED AROUND A WIDE RANGE
OF PRINCIPLES.[6]

This place, this special place, makes the people drink and
they sometimes fall out onto the street. And you wonder
when they fall on the street, whether that moment of falling
is actually something that they ever anticipate, consider,
contemplate, or practice. What are they thinking? Heading
for a small kitchen, someone comes in through the back
door and finds the boss sitting there and of course offers
him a drink. And so he has a drink again, for the last time.
And this, of course, leads him back to that moment of falling
out of the building; it leads to a moment when everything
started to end. But then again it could be said to be the only
time when something was really working in this situation,
when something was working in the factory, the only factory.
The factory that didn't qualify for economic packages
because it only made individual things. So you have to think
about what's missing and you have to think about this idea,
this misused phrase that came up a couple of days ago. The
theory boom. Not here, but somewhere else, because it's
not a theory boom that we are talking about but a difference
between making and receiving. What have you got? What
do you want? When can I get it? When do you want it? Why
isn't it working? Why are you not working? Maybe it's a lack

of excess analysis. You could say that the communal environment is one where a situation is created that is connected to an excess of analysis. Rooted in a collective effort at examining the idea of what has been produced in relation to an outside world, which must always exist, to be worked against.

Trying to protect the conditions in which it might be possible to produce something that people do not know that they want without giving up the idea that this might lead to improvement. Simultaneously trying out an idea that for things to be better you have to involve planning. It's an elegantly executed last-ditch swan-dive against speculative ideas. The theory boom could be renamed the assessment boom or the analysis boom. The idea of a situation where people develop an increasing separation of the thing they are trying to deal with and the way in which that thing has been discussed. Something is missing in that special factory where the man is making one thing at a time in a neo-industrial situation. It lacks an overdose of analysis; it lacks the logical progression of communal mentality. A situation originally positioned as a better lifestyle, a better place, a less alienating place, involves a lifestyle focus. The idea of making better trays to collect your lunch on, the idea of making a better place to relax in. The idea of having a pool table where you can hang out and do post- and pre-work. (That bit is endemic in this bar-strewn environment.) That last place, that place where people are actually building individual hovercrafts and wondering why no one wants to buy them. Lacking an excess of analysis and the analysis of potential. Not a bad product. It's a world situation.

PART 7

YOU ARE TO BE DRAWN ON A HURDLE THROUGH THE CITY OF LONDON TO TYBURN, THERE TO BE HANGED TILL YOU BE HALF DEAD, AFTER THAT CUT DOWN YET ALIVE, YOUR BOWELS TO BE TAKEN OUT OF YOUR BODY AND BURNED BEFORE YOU, YOUR PRIVY PARTS CUT OFF, YOUR HEAD CUT OFF, YOUR BODY TO BE DIVIDED IN FOUR PARTS, AND YOUR HEAD AND BODY TO BE SET AT SUCH PLACES AS THE KING SHALL ASSIGN.[7]

The last speaker is ready and smiles before speaking. "You have to imagine a man who was encouraged to pray every day to St Thomas More, a man who was encouraged to pray in order to save a soul for Thomas More. Thomas More who this week became the patron saint of politicians. Thomas More who finally, after nearly 500 years, has something to be a saint for and an activity to be saint of. Thomas More went to Belgium. Thomas More discussed a lot of issues with emergent humanist thinkers.

"The monastery at La Tourette near Lyon in France has a Thomas More Centre for Research. It is supposed to look at ethics and moral constructions and the conscience of politics. Conscience within the strategy of quasi-governmental organisations. La Tourette is a building by Le Courbusier. It's not so old; in monastery terms it is disturbingly new. Yet it has a Thomas More Centre. The trial of Thomas More leads up to a question of conscience, refusing to take part and saying: 'I cannot answer your question'. It's a very important moment, it's an important gesture to make Thomas More a patron saint of politicians. He was the politician not the saint. Thomas More was a politician within a religious context. He said he couldn't answer a very precise question because it was a question of conscience. It was not a question that could be asked, it was a question that had to remain part of an internal dialogue. Invoking conscience is a defence of irritation. He was killed, but first he was threatened with a triple death in brutalised forms. An irritating defence, an irritating way of getting out of answering a question. The creation of the question of conscience. So no reply, just bring him a chair.

In certain social circumstances there is a desire to shift the centre of power from one location to the other and back again, while killing someone at least twice. Sending them home in a taxi with their eyeballs in their lap, and making their family pay for the eventual bullet.

"A bar in a small island-state overlooked by an army checkpoint. Overlooked by silent soldiers but still a place to go and have a drink. Where people are determined to stay late and make a point. They say that something is going on here that is beyond an idea of conflict. They say it is a demonstration of social behaviour, a demonstration of being in a bar in a small island-state. The bar is normal inside and looks like a dinged up concrete bunker from the outside. They are saying that the idea of a bar in a small island-state in clear view of an army checkpoint is an essential demonstration of play. It's an essential demonstration that you can't organise a certain form of social organisation.

"Driving to a bar, a journey that takes eighteen hours through the fog. Arriving at a place where it snows rarely but it has today and where the driver and companion consequently think that there will always be a good chance of at least a sprinkling. Thinking and driving the day before HOTEL CALIFORNIA is released. The bar will never be the same again. Once HOTEL CALIFORNIA has arrived they'll be humming it for years. Sitting on a Spanish toilet, reading the paper as the Flamenco muzak reveals an Eagle-esque basis. A projection of another place. The bar in that small island-state stays resolutely silent; there is no music in this bar, no records to play. It's only a place for telling stories in modulated tones. It's a place for demonstrating that you can overlook the idea of social organisation but you won't stop people buying chips on the way home. It's a bar where if you have a certain accent it is necessary to repeat your name in order to explain to the other people in the bar that your recent arrival is all towards taking part in demonstrations of lounging and resistance. Believe strongly in one side, not the other. Even if they are not articulating it they are demonstrating it by their very presence in the place.
"There is someone else in the bar, who has to think about

Thomas More every night. He talks about ideas around conscience. He uses the idea of 'I am not going tell you', as a defence of irritation. He thinks about exceptionalism, as in, 'That's all very well, but we are considering exceptional circumstances.' And this bar, it has to work, it has to be solid, and it has to be constructed. When the doors move they have to be part of a special hydraulic mechanism. They can't just be just slid open by a gaffer, best-boy or stage-hand.

"And of course, it makes you think about an old man watching Italy versus the rest of the world on Eurosport. Watching an old man, just sitting there slumped over sideways watching Italy take on all the others in a war of defensive attrition. And there are small children again. Maybe it is a projection of the earlier commune but now distracted by the scene of a group of children sitting at the feet of an old man who is watching Italy play itself into the ground."

PART 8

WE ARE NOT, I BELIEVE, BOUND TO DECIDE. AN INTERPRETIVE
DECISION DOES NOT HAVE TO DRAW A LINE BETWEEN TWO
INTENTS OR TWO POLITICAL CONTENTS. OUR INTERPRETATIONS
WILL NOT BE READINGS OF A HERMENEUTIC OR EXEGETIC
SORT, BUT RATHER POLITICAL INTERVENTIONS IN THE
POLITICAL REWRITING OF THE TEXT AND ITS DESTINATION.
THIS IS THE WAY IT HAS ALWAYS BEEN—AND ALWAYS IN A
SINGULAR MANNER—FOR EXAMPLE, EVER SINCE WHAT IS
CALLED THE END OF PHILOSOPHY, AND BEGINNING WITH THE
TEXTUAL INDICATOR NAMED 'HEGEL'. THIS IS NO ACCIDENT.
IT IS AN EFFECT OF THE DESTINATIONAL STRUCTURE OF ALL
SO-CALLED POST-HEGELIAN TEXTS. THERE CAN ALWAYS BE A
HEGELIANISM OF THE LEFT AND A HEGELIANISM OF THE RIGHT,
A HEIDEGGERIANISM OF THE LEFT AND A HEIDEGGERIANISM
OF THE RIGHT, A NIETZSCHEANISM OF THE RIGHT AND
A NIETZCHEANISM OF THE LEFT, AND EVEN, LET US NOT
OVERLOOK IT, A MARXISM OF THE RIGHT AND A MARXISM OF
THE LEFT. THE ONE CAN ALWAYS BE THE OTHER, THE DOUBLE
OF THE OTHER. [8]

But we've got a problem here, we've got excess of
something, we've got this construction of conscience
directed towards certain locations by a small group of people
who appear to be problematic in terms of their avoidance of
the reconstruction of a peculiarly contemporary form of
ethical collapse. You have a post-planning form of
conscience circling around something more stable. You have
a communal model pitched against the idea of politicians
praying. You have a monastic construction. And perfect
building. A place where people go to sit and think about the
ethics and the built terminology of moral behaviour. So to
the moment of transmission. Sitting in a greenroom now.
Waiting for the first section of three transmissions.

Reviewing COUSIN. A local view. Encompassing micro-
community. Not established but operating under conditions
of micro-morality. Free-flowing around an embryonic set of
collective conditions played out through the actions of
offspring. A local viewing. An experiment for people involved

in transmission and exchange. Waiting under the same conditions, enduring some daily renewable social collapse. Localised structure affects behaviour while tweaking development. Post-presentation is relaxing our group. Post-presentation analysis with a sense of punishment. Self-punishment and reconstruction. And the neighbourhood view is different to the local view. COUSIN is like a village view, not with precision, but in a post-communal form, a small bungalow sitting by an ancient feature. It's a place that remains located, that remains fixed, it remains in place yet it is a reflection of other neighbourhoods that have everything except the silhouette of earlier cyclical near-stasis.

BAR. It's a place where some people arrive out of the blue, the day before HOTEL CALIFORNIA is released, and there must be a way of talking about this record arriving, there must be a way to talk about the idea of a bar, to confer some positions as signs of judgement. We have to encompass aspiration and desire and belief, it cannot be a critique.

PRICE is set in a greenroom and the greenroom is the perfect location. A greenroom painted beige. The part of a television studio where you wait. A place where you go before you present, and a place where you go after presentation. It's the place where you have an internalised party of relief, where you are nervous, where you are fine, where you are relieved, where you plan, where you have the argument after the debate, where you have the potential before the exchange, where you are not given the questions. It's the perfect place—t's the location where people circulate around the present. It's the place that brings together those who do not want to talk to each other. A true place of debate that may be the perfect model. If you are looking for three ways to articulate revised forms of moral and ethical behaviour without looking at a model of globalisation or questions of aesthetics, maybe it is necessary to look towards the multiplied localised view, the neighbourhood view within a reflected other place, this greenroom, this room just before and just after the moment of exchange.

PART 9

THE CITY IS BAD, FOR THERE IS MONEY IN THE CITY. PEOPLE
CAN BE REFORMED BUT NOT CITIES. BY SWEATING TO CLEAR
THE LAND, SOW AND HARVEST CROPS, MEN WILL LEARN THE
REAL VALUE OF THINGS. MAN HAS TO KNOW THAT HE IS BORN
FROM A GRAIN OF RICE!

EVERYTHING MUST BE CLEAR BETWEEN US, EVERYONE MUST
KNOW EVERYONE ELSE AS WELL AS THE IMAGE OF HIS OWN
FACE REFLECTED IN THE MIRROR.

SHOULD THE PEOPLE REST, OR NOT? ACCORDING TO OUR
OBSERVATIONS, WORKING WITHOUT ANY REST AT ALL IS BAD
FOR THE HEALTH. THERE'S NOT ENOUGH FOOD FOR PEOPLE
TO WORK ALL THE TIME; AND LEISURE INCREASES ONE'S
STRENGTH. IF A PERSON DOESN'T REST, HE GETS VERY ILL. IT
IS A STRATEGIC OBJECTIVE TO INCREASE THE STRENGTH OF
THE PEOPLE. THEREFORE, LEISURE MUST BE CONSIDERED TO
BE BASIC.

DON'T TRY TO ESCAPE BY MAKING PRETEXTS—ACCORDING
TO YOUR HYPOCRITICAL IDEAS. IT IS STRICTLY FORBIDDEN TO
CONTEST ME. DO SIT DOWN QUIETLY. WAIT FOR THE ORDERS.
IF THERE ARE NO ORDERS, DO NOTHING. IF I ASK YOU TO
DO SOMETHING, YOU MUST IMMEDIATELY DO IT WITHOUT
PROTESTING.[9]

So we are looking at an examination of shifting concepts of
conscience and ethics. And it might be necessary to change
the scene. To cut away to some external activity. Attention
shifts across time as we track the stories of six
supplementary people who come together at various points
during their research into the participants of a commune.
Their work evolves in three separate cities and in each one a
series of passing moments is about to take place towards a
revision of ethics and strategy in relation to the development
and growth of these different urban locations. The six people
involved pass each other at various points in the narrative as
they develop their presentations and refine other people's
arguments. Yet we are never permitted access to their

specific detailed experience. Only a complex world of relationships and negotiations.

Towards the end we shift to three distinctive narrative sections based on three radio plays that are heard in passing by those involved at specific uncoordinated moments. COUSIN, BAR, PRICE. There is some additional rejigging of the narrative play which must exist if there is any attempt to grasp the slippery constructions at hand and play is the correct description here, as something more precise will not do. Any attempt to address the idea of how to behave is going to be connected to ideas about judgement. Yet construction of judgements in situations has become elusive. The elusiveness that is under consideration here is not terminal, it doesn't disappear but remains hard to pin down at all times. It is a fragmented form of elusiveness. The issue is how to define the idea of reassessment within a set of conditions where such reassessment has become a fetish, where precision is constantly being reformulated. A suspension of judgement and a concurrent restriction on the application of terms of conscience. There is always the suspended judgement moment where there emerges a constant play with short-term time management and concurrent short-term ethical reconfiguration. Yet what route do such concepts of conscience take? Where do these new forms of conscience come from? Who is designing these new ethical forms? (While you are sitting watching a report that shows, with pride, old footage of a barrel being dropped from a boat onto an inflatable craft.) That change, that shift of conscience, the man sitting in Amsterdam, talking about advertising, repossessing the language of creativity and vision, using this flexibility, using suspended judgements, yet overstating them, not in freedom, not in liberty, none of these things, but within an idea of visioning some more ways to see some more visions. A coquettish appropriation of the concept of having an idea of what might take place when you can no longer unravel presentation, judgement and desire.

PART 10

COMMUNICATION, AS MUCH AS IT APPEARS TO RUN FREE, IS IN FACT REINED IN. DURING THE 1960s, WHEN TELEVISION APPEARED ON THE CULTURAL SCENE AS A NEW PHENOMENON, A CERTAIN NUMBER OF 'SOCIOLOGISTS' (QUOTATION MARKS NEEDED HERE) RUSHED TO PROCLAIM THAT, AS A 'MEANS OF MASS COMMUNICATION', TELEVISION WAS GOING TO 'MASSIFY' EVERYTHING. IT WAS GOING TO BE THE GREAT LEVELLER AND TURN ALL VIEWERS INTO ONE BIG, UNDIFFERENTIATED MASS. IN FACT, THIS ASSESSMENT SERIOUSLY UNDERESTIMATED A VIEWER'S CAPACITY FOR RESISTANCE. BUT ABOVE ALL, IT UNDERESTIMATED TELEVISION'S ABILITY TO TRANSFORM ITS VERY PRODUCERS AND THE OTHER JOURNALISTS THAT COMPETE WITH IT AND, ULTIMATELY, THROUGH ITS IRRESISTIBLE FASCINATION FOR SOME OF THEM, THE ENSEMBLE OF CULTURAL PRODUCERS. THE MOST IMPORTANT DEVELOPMENT, AND A DIFFICULT ONE TO FORESEE, WAS THE EXTRAORDINARY EXTENSION OF THE POWER OF TELEVISION OVER THE WHOLE OF CULTURAL PRODUCTION, INCLUDING SCIENTIFIC AND ARTISTIC PRODUCTION.[10]

Sitting in a greenroom, thinking of possibilities. Thinking of how to present. Content has become crushed within the thought process. Reflection and anticipation are melded. Is there a way to work around the moment of presentation? Is there a way to use some stories and some description, to drop in moments of evidence as a way to keep a distance from the central event? The interior is straightforward, both in terms of idea and location. The colour and design are not thought through. The intensity of anticipation and relief overwrite any problem or question about the nature of this place. Someone is thinking. There are other people in the room too and they are all heading in different directions. Thinking in parallel, wondering about some other scenarios that will constantly distract them from the moment and shift things to the 'just before' and 'just after'. Thinking aloud about some trickle of extended action. Moments that are suspended without resolution or completion.

So you need some details within a postscript. There are some little fragments that are worth bringing up. There is a man seen standing by a subway entrance. It's late at night and we are in a city to the west of an island. The location is not a bad one and the subway entrance emerges right by a convenience store. The space appears to be an all-night shop and offers some promise. Yet any entrance to the place would be stifled by the reality of a non-choice on offer.

There is some packaging and some products, each one chosen to provide a barely sufficient array of primary things, yet the choice of each item seems somehow arbitrary. There is a particular notebook, there is a thing best used to make holes in paper, there is one type of soup and there are ten kinds of birthday candle. A sense of managed arbitrary choice that is overwhelming. None of the things have an equivalent quality or value. The 'managed arbitrary' is constantly bounced back at the browser of the store who knows that each choice of the goods on offer has been made with some care about the idea of making a choice about goods to offer. This apparent arbitrary hyper-choice at the store has something to do with short-time projection and is somehow connected to an idea of suspended judgement. The total achievement in this situation is abstract in the sense that it eludes most attempts at logical analysis. The range of items on offer in this particular store is one fragment of something. The range seems to be a reflection of pressures or experiments. It's unclear if the choice is due to laziness, due to compression of time and resources or due to experiments at shifting as many candles as possible. It's not unreasonable to suppose that this is not a store organised by an individual. It is owned by an organised projected strategic organisation and it is an attempt at logical analysis but the result is one of complex interplay of language, supply and expansion. This apparently particular/arbitrary set of choices is not entirely controlled by cost, analysis, cost/benefit analysis, supply or exhaustion. Neutral risk that carries a shadow of choice. It's possible that it is a true game, fundamental things are provided that could be useful for any passing traveller or it could be a repository of things to buy due to the stress of dislocation. Three layers of highways cross here, a perfect place for an earthquake. A woman sits alone at the bar across the street. Close by another man is sleeping while his telephone rings. Three people sit together some distance away while the woman nods forward and draws increasingly small circles with her finger on the wet wood of the bar. The people working in the bar have to step down to serve you. Everyone else sits at the counter. The people working at the bar are standing yet their heads are at the same height as the seated patrons. The floor area of the bar is lower than the floor area of the rest of the place. Yes, the barmen are situated at exactly the right height to deal with everyone sitting at the bar, but the wrong height when viewed in relation to the room as a whole. Super short, but with perfectly proportioned heads. The woman sitting at the bar is completely and utterly drunk and her dress is made out of artificial fibres. She turns while holding a medium-sized metal spoon (used for what exactly? Super-size the martini?) which she hurls towards the three people sitting across the room. And they feel the rush as it tumbles past them towards some clanking against the wooden panelling of the wall. Of course sometimes it is better to act as if something just fell from the sky.

There is a delay before the woman is hustled out of the bar. A bar close to the subway station where the man emerged from the convenience store. A twenty-four-hour shop where everyone is really sorry for troubling you, and simultaneously really concerned and really happy to see you. And there is this drunk woman at the bar wearing a dress made of artificial fibre, throwing a spoon across the room and no one is doing anything and no one is saying anything until she is jumped upon by a number of officials from the hotel who drag her physically out of the bar, past three people who have merely sensed something fall from the sky. Then apology. Overstated and excessive. A question of behaviour and embarrassment and apology and denial in three short stories that feel like radio plays. A flash across from one set of apparently developed, successful conditions to another. An understanding of the application of attitudes to business, attitudes to modern developed production techniques and the effect that this mentality has had on ways of working.

There has to be some consideration of all this over a last drink.

And the woman at the bar is not perfect but there is something about her throwing spoons while someone else sleeps that heats up situations to the point where it might be possible to rethink attitudes towards exchange. More specifically about the replacement of one paternalistic system with a more metaphysical and in Judeo-Christian terms, paganistic nature-logic system of exchange. And this is not a value judgement, it is just something to lock onto and it comes down to the look, it comes down to aesthetics. It comes down to a point where there might be a way to play with the revised aesthetic of revised ethical structure. Is it possible to talk about a sense of abstraction pitched up against 'The Patron Saint of Politicians?' Is it possible to think about the man who said: "I can't answer that pragmatic political question because it's a question of conscience"? Who emphasised the individual in the face of organisation? Is it possible to grasp the definitive expressions of shifts in conscience and ethics as they are taking place yet while people feel exactly the opposite is happening—it must be possible within a structure like this. Literally no place is a way of writing the word utopia in another form. Literally no place cannot substitute for utopia. Utopia is literally no place. It's critique, it's not vision. A critique of humanistic thinking. Yet here is the man who said, "I can't answer that question because it's a question of conscience." How do you play with this legacy and how do you play with the legacy of shift and effect? Reflecting back onto a European base. Revised business strategies and business practice. Can you play with shifts and appropriation of conscience and how those things manifest themselves, how they find form? What are the semiotics of the visualisation of replayed and reclaimed moments of conscience and ethical behaviour, especially when people feel exactly the opposite is taking place? Strike breaking and joining the army, video games where you have to sneak up on other people and kill them. No more head-on. Just walk around and slit some throats and walk away again. Final exchange.

Later that night the commune is quiet and the looping revisitors are sitting in the eating place. Well-designed trays are stacked up next to wooden salad bowls. One of the diners asks to borrow a jacket. He has a cigarette in his hand, which has nearly burned down to the stub. Turning to the other people at the table he asks them to think of a simple shape. No one really wants to pay attention but out of some mumbled response a cross is decided upon. So a small cross is drawn on the glowing cigarette end. Grasping the jacket from below, he creates a fist wrapped in cloth. A jacket over a hand, a hand wrapped in cloth. Carefully he inserts the cigarette into a hollow created by the wrapped fingers while, with a lowering of voices the friends start to take notice. Holding attention now towards a moment of precision. There is a pause while we wait for the smell of burning cloth. Focused and a little drunk he begins to remove the jacket from his hand and to collective brow flickers of strained surprise the cigarette has gone. Sitting back down at the table he is now surrounded by the semi-impressed. Let that hold, let it ride. Wait for the turn away. As the first breaks to restart the talk, a moment crystalises. The cigarette man starts to convulse and wretch, bending low. Coughing, gagging and hacking. A stub, a short stub, wet with spit lands on the tabletop, now soiled with strings of tobacco lumped together the barely stable paper and filter. And clearly drawn on its side is a small cross.

Now the group are smiling with ease, they are happy to play and stop playing with each other. Turning away they start talking once more with fresh animation but are tangled up again in mid-flow. There is something else in his mouth. Turning now they see him produce a second wet cigarette end, then a third and then a fourth. We have reached a point where the table is covered in spittled tobacco and paper. Each stump carrying a different tiny drawing: a square, a circle, a squiggle, a triangle, a diamond. General. Predicted, if you think about it. Guessable. Limited. But beyond some tricks and towards a realm of unexpected yet predictable options.

EPILOGUE

THE LIVING QUARTERS AND DAILY SCHEDULES OF THE OLDER
CHILDREN FURNISHED A PARTICULARLY GOOD EXAMPLE
OF BEHAVIOURAL ENGINEERING. AT FIRST SIGHT THEY
SEEMED WHOLLY CASUAL, ALMOST HAPHAZARD, BUT AS
FRAZIER POINTED OUT THEIR SIGNIFICANT FEATURES AND
THE CONSEQUENCES OF EACH, I BEGAN TO MAKE OUT A
COMPREHENSIVE, ALMOST MACHIAVELLIAN DESIGN.

THE CHILDREN PASSED SMOOTHLY FROM ONE AGE GROUP TO
ANOTHER, FOLLOWING A NATURAL PROCESS OF GROWTH AND
AVOIDING THE ABRUPT CHANGES OF THE HOME-AND-SCHOOL
SYSTEM. THE ARRANGEMENTS WERE SUCH THAT EACH CHILD
EMULATED CHILDREN SLIGHTLY OLDER THAN HIMSELF AND
HENCE DERIVED MOTIVES AND PATTERNS FOR MUCH OF HIS
EARLY EDUCATION WITHOUT ADULT AID. [11]

THE MIDDLE IS BY NO MEANS AN AVERAGE; ON THE CONTRARY,
IT IS WHERE THINGS PICK UP SPEED. 'BETWEEN' THINGS
DOES NOT DESIGNATE A LOCALISABLE RELATION GOING
FROM ONE THING TO THE OTHER AND BACK AGAIN, BUT A
PERPENDICULAR DIRECTION, A TRANSVERSAL MOVEMENT THAT
SWEEPS ONE 'AND' THE OTHER AWAY, A STREAM WITHOUT
BEGINNING OR END THAT UNDERMINES ITS BANKS AND PICKS
UP SPEED IN THE MIDDLE.

EVEN THE MOST STRIATED CITY GIVES RISE TO SMOOTH
SPACES: TO LIVE IN THE CITY AS A NOMAD, OR AS A CAVE
DWELLER. MOVEMENTS, SPEED AND SLOWNESS, ARE
SOMETIMES ENOUGH TO RECONSTRUCT A SMOOTH SPACE.
OF COURSE, SMOOTH SPACES ARE NOT IN THEMSELVES
LIBERATORY. BUT THE STRUGGLE IS CHANGED OR DISPLACED
IN THEM, AND LIFE RECONSTITUTES ITS STAKES, CONFRONTS
NEW OBSTACLES, INVENTS NEW PACES, SWITCHES
ADVERSARIES. NEVER BELIEVE THAT A SMOOTH SPACE WILL
SUFFICE TO SAVE US. [12]

Their minds are now clear. Potential and complication are
written over each other. Perfect information combined with
an excess of options. Contained within an array of

possibilities that will allow them to continue for at least one more day. They will turn in the ravine and climb to the top of a bank, just to see the place again. Going for three days, they will walk more than one hundred kilometres. It will feel like half that distance and may be double. Some of the group will be reluctant to leave at first and happy to realise that the route is now direct. There will be precise purpose over the next few days, walking and thinking and moving. No lack of focus but productive working processes turned away from themselves. There will be a strong desire to keep walking and to press on beyond the mountains. They will always speak, always plan together, they will never allow themselves to swing in an arc. Shifting away had been the only option anyway. The last car left some time ago and the only remaining truck had a transmission completely drained of fluid that whined and screeched even when they tried to improvise some lubrication with home improved hydraulic fluid. So they will always set off on foot. Hot feet held by frayed footwear and towards the end, no shoes at all.

NOTES

(1) County Magistrate, Mr Broughton Charlton speaking as chairman of a meeting held at the Assembly Rooms, Nottingham on 14 January 1860, reported in THE DAILY TELEGRAPH of 17 January 1860 and quoted by Karl Marx in CAPITAL, volume 1, Everyman's Library edition, 1930.

(2) Theodore Adorno, 'Resignation', from THE CULTURE INDUSTRY, Routledge, London, 1991.

(3) Marc Augé, NON-PLACES: INTRODUCTION TO AN ANTHROPOLOGY OF SUPERMODERNITY, Verso, London, 1995.

(4) Gilles Deleuze, CINEMA 1: THE MOVEMENT IMAGE, The Athlone Press, London, 1992.

(5) Paul Virilio, OPEN SKY, Verso, London, 1997.

(6) Martin Shaw, 'The Theoretical Challenge of Global Society', in Sreberny-Mohhammadi, Winseck, McKenna and Boyd-Barrett (eds.), MEDIA IN GLOBAL CONTEXT, Edward Arnold, London, 1994 (extract from 'Global Society and International Relations').

(7) Collated by Peter Ackroyd in THE LIFE OF THOMAS MORE, 1998, from the following sources: William Roper, 'The Life of Sir Thomas More', in Richard S. Sylvester and David P. Harding (eds.), TWO EARLY TUDOR LIVES, Yale University Press, New Haven, 1963; E. Reynolds, THE TRIAL OF SAINT THOMAS MORE, Burns & Oates, London, 1964; J. D. M. Derrett, 'The Trial of Thomas More', in THE GUILDHALL MISCELLANY, London, 1963; R. W. Chambers, THOMAS MORE, Vintage, London, 1998.

(8) Jacques Derrida, THE EAR OF THE OTHER: OTOBIOGRAPHY, Transference, Translation, University of Nebraska Press, Lincoln NE, 1988.

(9) Various statements attributed to members of the Khmer Rouge, including Pol Pot and Kang Kek Ieu.

(10) Pierre Bourdieu, ON TELEVISION AND JOURNALISM, Pluto Press, London, 1998.

(11) BF Skinner, WALDEN 2, Macmillan, London, 1948.

(12) Gilles Deleuze and Felix Guattari, A THOUSAND PLATEAUS: CAPITALISM AND SCHIZOPHRENIA, Athlone Press, London, 1988.

ACKNOWLEDGEMENTS TO PUBLISHERS

ERAMSUS IS LATE
Published by Book Works, London, 1995, second edition 2000
Edited by Jane Rolo, English edition
88 pages, black and white, soft cover with laser-cut title
180 x 115 mm
Illustrations by Gillian Gillick, designed by Rose-Innes Associates
ISBN 978 1 870699 17 4
ERASME EST EN RETARD
Published by les presses du réel, Dijon, 1997
Translated by Philippe Parreno, French edition
64 pages, black and white, soft cover
240 x 170 mm
ISBN 978 2 84066 003 3

IBUKA!
Published by Künstlerhaus Stuttgart, 1995
Edited by Nicholas Schafhausen, English / German edition
66 pages, black and white, soft cover
180 x 135 mm
Designed by Justus Köhncke
No ISBN

THE WINTER SCHOOL
Published by JRP, Geneva, 1996
Edited by Lionel Bovier and Christophe Cherix
2-colour offset print, edition 200
420 x 594mm
Designed by Liam Gillick
No ISBN

DISCUSSION ISLAND / BIG CONFERENCE CENTRE
Published by Kunstverein Ludwigsburg and the Orchard Gallery Derry, 1997
Edited by Barbara Steiner and Liam Kelly, English / German edition
200 pages, black and white, soft cover
180 x 130 mm
Designed by Liam Gillick, cover image by Sarah Morris
No ISBN
L'ÎLE DE LA DISCUSSION/LE GRAND CENTRE DE CONFÉRENCE
Published by les presses du réel, Dijon, 1998
French edition
100 pages, black and white, soft cover
240 x 170 mm
ISBN 978 2 84066 028 6

MCNAMARA
The text formed a central part of the exhibition McNamara,
Schipper & Krome, Cologne, 1994
Three additional, unique versions were subsequently written
An extract was published as part of a publication also comprising extracts
from ERASMUS AND IBUKA! REALISATIONS AND THE WHAT IF? SCENARIOS
Published by Le Consortium, Dijon and Kunstverein Hamburg, 1997
Edited by Eric Troncy, English / French edition
112 pages, black and white and colour, soft cover
215 x 153 mm
Designed by Liam Gillick
No ISBN

LITERALLY NO PLACE
Published by Book Works, London, 2002
Edited by Jane Rolo and Maria Fusco, English edition
72 pages, two colours, soft cover
179 x 130 mm
Designed by Liam Gillick and Silke Roch
ISBN 978 1 870699 66 2

ALL BOOKS
Liam Gillick

Published and distributed by Book Works, London

ISBN 978 1 906012 17 5

Cover image by M/M (Paris) and Liam Gillick
Edited by Jane Rolo and Gerrie van Noord
Design by Liam Gillick, Book Works
Typeset by Claire Mason
Printing by Die Keure, Bruges

ALL BOOKS is published in an edition of 1,500 copies.
A limited edition of 30 unique copies has been signed
and numbered by the artist, with a special binding
designed and produced by Book Works.

Book Works is funded by Arts Council England and
this publication is generously supported by our
printers, Die Keure.

Opus Projects: Opus 6

Book Works
19 Holywell Row
London EC2A 4JB
www.bookworks.org.uk